Train to Win!
11 Principles of Athletic Success

By Martin Rooney

 First Edition

Address questions or comments to the following e-mail address: amlvma@aol.com

This book is written for the purposes of education and information. Before implementing any methods or techniques presented in this book, please consult your physician or a certified strength specialist. All forms of exercise present risk of injury, and the author cannot be held responsible.

Printed in Atlanta, Georgia, USA

The Parisi Speed School
2-22 Banta Place
Fair Lawn, NJ 07410
201-794-1555
parisischool.com

Acknowledgements

This book has taken over a year of my life to write, but the information covered within these pages has taken over thirty years to experience. Most of what is written is not novel, but expansions of the lessons given to me by so many people in my life.

I wish to thank the following people for their kind assistance:

Amanda Rooney, my wife, without her loving patience and support this book would never have happened.

Luca Atalla, Editor Gracie Magazine, he is a great man that not only got me started writing this book, but showed me how to take on the world.

Bill Parisi, Owner Parisi Sports Clubs USA, my best friend and mentor, he gave me a chance to realize what it is to do what you really love.

Walt Andzel, Professor, Kean University, he is one of the originators in our great field, he gave me direction and criticism to bring this book to life.

Ricardo Almeida, Jiu Jitsu Black Belt, my brother, he has taught me more about myself in recent years than anyone I know, I look forward to the rest of the journey.

Joe DeFranco, Performance Enhancement Specialist, my most respected colleague, without him constantly pushing me to be better, I would not be where I am today.

John Derent, Sports Science Specialist, one of the oldest friends I have, he has been superb research consultant, always leading me in the right direction.

Dave Tate, Owner, Elite Fitness Systems, one of the strongest guys I know, not only physically, but influentially in our field as well.

Finally, I would also like to thank my family, my friends, my coworkers and all my past teachers and coaches for giving me the tools to make this book possible. The greatest teachers of all are the athletes themselves. Without their hopes and dreams, there would be nothing for me to write about at all.

Table of Contents

CHAPTER 1

What is Principle Centered Training?

Secondary to the luxury of training at the Parisi Speed School, one of the top facilities in the country, I have had the opportunity to hold court with many of the top trainers in the world. Interestingly, a common question trainers have for one another is, "What is your training philosophy?" There are usually very distinct, rehearsed answers. The answers are also quite different, which forces these elite trainers to stand by and defend their philosophy of training. I have watched fights almost break out due to the reverence some of these trainers hold for their ideals. Unfortunately, these "philosophies" are not always well thought out or well supported. Often these scripts are "handed down to the next" without full experience with other methods. There are also the philosophies that cater to the newest, trendiest ideas in the training arena. These trainers are placing their methods at the center of their thought and using this center to make their decisions about training. If the only tool I think about is a hammer, then everything is going to look like a nail, even if it is not the correct tool to use at the time.

A great parable I often use to illustrate this method-centered philosophy begins with a man that has to cross a river. He cannot swim, so he has to find the best method for crossing the river at that particular time. Finally, he settles on a raft, and the raft safely gets him across the river. He is then convinced that the raft is the greatest invention ever, and carries the raft everywhere he goes once on dry land. He begins to find that carrying the raft is making life harder, but he is not prepared to change. He is then known as "the guy with the raft," and he begins to like his distinction. He tries to convince everyone that life is not complete without a raft, and that bikes, cars and planes

are not the way to travel. He continues this way the rest of his life, but never sees that he is centered around the raft instead of the principles of why he used the raft in the first place.

When I answer the questions about my training philosophy, I tell people I use a **Principle Centered Approach**. Over the last 15 years of training, learning, teaching and coaching, I have been on a personal mission to seek out the truths about training. At first, I only looked at methodologies that I considered the best. For instance, is "HIT" training (single set to failure) better than multiple sets? Is higher rep training better than lower rep ranges? What about the Big Three (bench, squat, deadlift) versus the Olympic lifts (snatch, clean and jerk)? Every method can have the strongest supporters and the strictest critics. I concluded that no method would ever be unanimously accepted as the best way to train. I knew, however, that training is a science, so there had to be sound scientific principles or truths that every method had to adhere to. This book is a reflection of my findings. These principles that are discussed are the Center Foundation Principles from which all purposeful training must be derived. These principles never change with time. Because of this these principles, I can create a guideline for optimal training. Think of these principles as the compass that will guide your way through the thick forest of training methods. If any of these principles are violated, then the methodology will not produce optimal results.

Most philosophy is not developed, but it is a training script taken from someone else. I see these scripts in action every day. Whether it is static stretching minutes before the big game, or an entire team following the exact same program, many of the principles contained in this text are not being followed. By centering your training around these

principles, and then applying them to your training, you can then form your own philosophy.

Even though honesty, commitment, determination, focus, and compassion are human principles that people know they should center themselves around, it doesn't always occur. Many of the principles included in this text are going to be very familiar. The true power occurs when you go from understanding them to living them. This is the challenge that this text gives you.

Begin by asking yourself if you are carrying any "rafts" around. If you are, try to leave it behind, but never forget what it did for you. You may someday have to cross a similar river again, and the old raft will be of great use. Grow from your experience, don't limit yourself with it.

CHAPTER 2

Required Characteristics for an Athlete

When I first began to write about what I considered to be the "true" principles of training, I thought that their complete description would be enough to lead students of training toward the "right" path. A mentor of mine, however, questioned me about what characteristics an athlete might first need to possess before any of the principles could be correctly put to use. This was the point when I began to develop the cyclical conceptual model that is going to be used throughout this book.

I have worked with many athletes that had all the talent in the world and never reached their potential, and I have also worked with less gifted athletes that went further than I could have ever hoped. Young or old, I began to realize that these successful athletes all possessed similar qualities that the less successful athletes did not.

I have often questioned whether an athlete is born of more genetic makeup or is it more environmental. This is the classic nature versus nurture question that is often asked during human development. Of the four essential qualities that I believe all successful athletes must possess, I believe that there is a combination of both genetics and environment at work. First, I believe an athlete must possess the characteristic of **honesty**. Whether this is one being honest with oneself, his family, coach or anyone, this quality cannot be missing to enjoy success. Second, **discipline** is mandatory to ever aspire to greatness. Without discipline, an athlete will be hard pressed to accomplish anything. Third, for an athlete to be disciplined, he must have a certain level of **mental toughness**. Without this ability to persevere in the face of adversity, discipline is impossible to maintain. Finally, an athlete must be able to **correctly respond to failure**.

Failure, or losing as it is seen in competition, is an essential event if growth and enhancement are ever to take place. Without having the ability to embrace and learn from past failures, the ability for an athlete to move forward will be severely limited.

The conceptual model pictured on the next page can be described as follows: First, an athlete must either possess or develop the four characteristics described above. Once these traits are demonstrated, this athlete has developed the core values upon which future work can be built. These core values can be seen as honesty, commitment, positive thinking, perseverance and growth. At this time, the athlete is prepared to apply the principles of training to his training philosophy. With the proper core values and an understanding of correct training principles in place, the athlete can now expect to experience training success and personal growth. As the old saying goes, "Success breeds success," these training enhancements as a result of proper athletic development will lead to further increases in one's athletic characteristics. The cycle can then continue over and over as the athlete continues to develop, learn and grow.

If the initial characteristics are not properly developed, weaker core values will result. Some of these could be dishonesty, quitting or stubbornness. When these values are applied to the principles of training, the system is sure to produce less than desirable results. Since the results are not adequate, the athlete can become discouraged and even give up on training completely. The remedy would be to adopt the proper athletic characteristics and begin again.

The first few chapters of this book are going to describe the essential characteristics of an athlete in more detail. Ask yourself as you are reading them how well your development in these areas is going. Think about what your core values are,

and if you are really living by them. Also think back on your training career to athletes that either did or did not have some of these characteristics. Then think about the consequences of both for them.

Cyclical Training Model

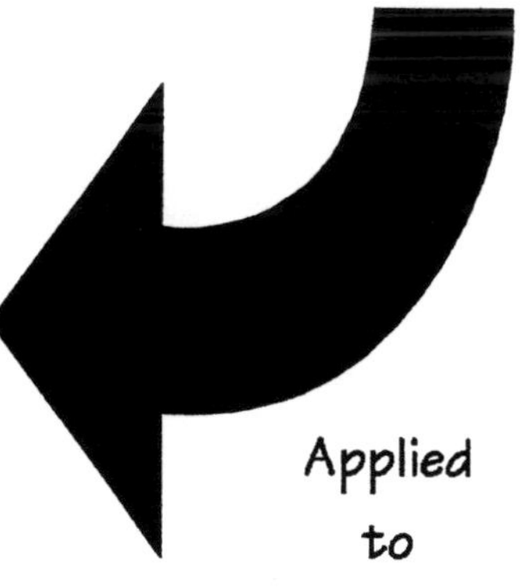

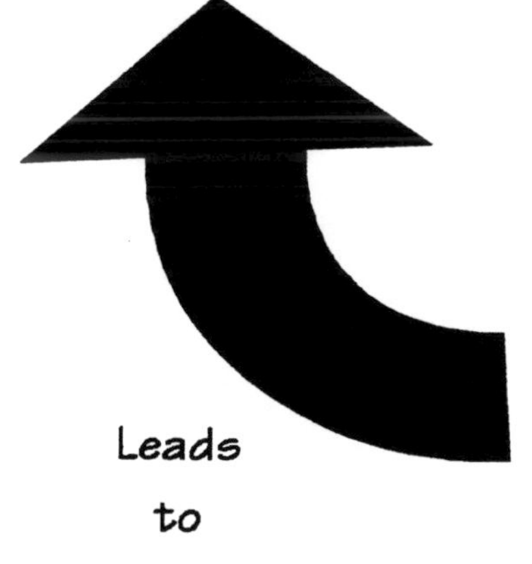

CHAPTER 3

Honesty is the Best Policy

My grandparents on my father's side were both teachers. While my father was growing up, he swore he would never teach. Today he owns a company that deals strictly with education. And he married my mother, also a teacher. I too never thought I wanted to be a teacher, but it is what I get enjoyment out of every day. I believe that everyone is a teacher in some way, and there are important lessons to learn from everything.

My father had a way of getting me to see right from wrong. A great example of this was a time during my senior year of high school. My friends were going to the beach and I wanted to go with them. At that time of the day, however, I had yet to mow the lawn as I had promised earlier. I put it off, and now I wanted to forget about the job completely. I had the pressure of a promise to my dad up against all my friends heading down to a fun day at the beach. When I presented him with the situation, he used his technique. "Do the right thing." Then I would explain how I could get to it later, or even tomorrow. "Do the right thing," he would counter. I would get angry and state that this wasn't fair. "Do the right thing." He would keep that up until I made my decision. That decision was to honor a promise and meet my friends later.

Being honest with yourself is probably one of the hardest things to do. Many find it difficult to make the right decisions or state things as they really are. To blame one's circumstances on outside forces is much easier than holding oneself responsible. To illustrate these ideas, I would like to quote James Allen in what I consider the best paragraph from his classic, As A Man Thinketh.

> "A man only begins to be a man when he ceases to whine and revile, and commences to search for the hidden justice which regulates his life. And as he adapts his mind to that regulating factor, he ceases to accuse others as the cause of his condition, and builds himself up in strong and noble thoughts; ceases to kick against circumstances, but begins to *use* them as aids to his more rapid progress, and as a means of discovering the hidden powers and possibilities within himself."

Being honest with yourself and accepting responsibility for your current situation is critical to future athletic success. Without this honesty, eventual problems are sure to arise.

Techniques to help improve your honesty with yourself would be to rate your efforts in all of your endeavors. I have heard so many athletes say that they "tried" their best in a certain event. When I ask them if it were a life or death situation instead of just training, could they have done more, the answer is always yes. This demonstrates to them that this was not their best effort. This dishonesty can eventually cause an athlete to let themselves down. When this occurs often enough, an athlete can find it hard to recover.

Another exercise I use to teach athletes about honesty is what I call my pen trick. I ask an athlete to "try" to take a pen out of my open hand. They usually smile, thinking I am going to pull away, and quickly rip the pen away. I then let them know that they did not follow directions. I said to "try" to take the pen. They went further than that and succeeded. They did take the pen. I hold the pen outstretched and ask them to "try"

again. This time they are more cautious, but may still remove the pen from my hand. At that point you repeat the exercise until they realize that when you try, nothing really happens. The pen stays in the hand and you have done nothing. So, when athletes tell me they are going to try to do a task, or try to get to their rehab, or try to finish the workout, I make sure to remind them of the terms they are using. They then replace the word "try" with "will," and hold themselves to their promise. When completed, their honesty to themselves has added a sweeter sense of accomplishment to what they have completed. In their minds, they have "Done the right thing."

A way that I have had the effects of dishonesty explained as it affects yourself and others is known as the "Iceberg Example." People and how they portray their honesty can be likened to an iceberg at sea. You may see a little bit of the iceberg exposed, but there is a huge mass of ice under the water that you cannot see. Just like the iceberg that sank the Titanic, it was this portion under the water that was most destructive. The portion under the water can be likened to the hidden inner turmoil that occurs when athletes are dishonest with themselves or others. This is exemplified by the great quote the famous boxer Joe Frazier, "If you cheated during your roadwork in that dark of the morning, you're getting found out now under the bright lights."

A coach of mine once told me that when you are honest, you don't have to remember anything. I believe this is true. I know this because as I have worked on my honesty, it has been a release from the inner turmoil that came along with the dishonesty. Once this turmoil is released, true growth can occur. Not just the growth of you personally, but the growth of the relationships of the coaches, athletes, and people around

you. When this level of honesty is in place, you are now ready to develop the other essential characteristics of an athlete.

CHAPTER 4

The Butterfly Called Discipline

Over the last ten years, I have had the luxury of working with a multitude of top level athletes in almost every sport one can imagine. From fighting to football, from bobsled to basketball, I have found that there are many attributes that all athletes must share to enjoy success. About a year ago, a World Cup soccer player I was training asked me what I believed to be the most important quality an athlete could possess. At first, a number of qualities came to mind, but when I really examined the question at length, I believe there is one quality that encompasses them all. This quality is discipline. Every other quality that an athlete can possess and nature must be done using the maximal amount of discipline. If the right amount of discipline is not present, every aspect of performance that it affects will eventually suffer. When I use the term "discipline," I am defining the term as control over yourself. You are the only one that can really let yourself down. When you lose discipline, or self control, usually less than desirable results occur. In this chapter I will give you some memorable tools to ensure that breakdowns in your discipline will happen as little as possible.

When I was an athlete on the US Bobsled team, there were a number of times I did not demonstrate the right amount of discipline. From missing a workout to going out partying to being late for meetings, I will not say I was ever perfect. Around this time, my father saw that I was not focusing myself as well as I could. That is when he introduced me to what in science is called **The Butterfly Effect**. The Butterfly Effect can best be described as the fact that nothing is predictable, and that enormous positive or negative effects can often be produced by very tiny causes. The example that is often used is that science has shown that the tiny flapping of a butterfly's wings in Japan could

lead to a monstrous storm in Brazil. So always keep in mind that as small as you think something is, it can have a huge positive or negative effect.

Now examine for a second the ways that you flap your wings each day when it comes to your training. Do you ever miss a workout? Do you always eat correctly? Do you push yourself as far as you need to go? The answers to all of these questions are most often no. Many athletes I have asked these questions usually say, "Who cares, I am only missing one workout" or "Don't worry, I will eat well tomorrow." But now let me illustrate the Butterfly Effect as it relates to discipline. Let's say that over a training period of 12 weeks leading up to a competition you miss 6 workouts which is only one every two weeks. Let us also say that you didn't eat well 20 of the 84 days of training. Then when the competition came, you were defeated because you narrowly lacked the strength and stamina needed for the win. Even though you felt you prepared, you now see how small breakdowns in discipline at the time lead to very big consequences. Understanding this, you must see that there are no small aspects to anything in training because tiny flaps of your wings can lead to a victory or defeat up to years from now. This knowledge should help you to sharpen your discipline so that you question the result of every decision you make about your training.

Another method to examine the Butterfly Effect and your discipline is a question I often ask my athletes, "How would you train if you knew this were your last competition?" Many answer that they would now attack every aspect of their training with a new overall zest for achievement. I am usually disappointed with this answer because it shows that none of the athletes believes that they are working as hard or as smart as they could. This further shows that there is a breakdown in their discipline

along the way in their training. What you must realize is that we only have a finite number of competitions and days to train, so you must treat each of those as if it were your last. If you are not living each workout to the fullest, you are not flapping your wings as hard as you could to cause great positive effects later.

An excellent way for athletes to attempt to examine their current level of discipline is what I call the **Discipline Curse**. After working with athletes for so long, I have also noticed a trend among most of them once their career was over. Most believe that their lack of discipline or knowledge did not allow them to achieve the level that they wanted. They can also usually pinpoint the times in their careers when this discipline was missing. I always tell my athletes that the worst feeling an athlete can be cursed with is the regret of looking back on their career and feeling empty because they could have done much more. If they knew their shortcomings then and regretted it, this means you can pinpoint your errors now to avoid the shortcomings that could haunt you later. No one is perfect; you are going to make mistakes and have breakdowns in your discipline. If you can minimize this as much as possible, great things are bound to happen. There will be good and bad days, just search for the lesson in each. Just make sure you are always looking to avoid the "Curse."

The final example I will use to demonstrate the importance of discipline is with the **Law of the Shark**. A shark, as we all know, must forever keep moving forward, or he cannot breathe and dies. Imagine the discipline that the shark has to possess. Perhaps there are days he wants to stop and take a rest, but this is not an option. You must attack your athletic career with the same determination. Just like the shark, you must constantly try to move forward. If you are not constantly bettering yourself, you are only staying the

same or getting worse. You must become disciplined enough to never let yourself stay at one level for too long. We all know there are going to be tough days. There are going to be times when that voice in your head says "Don't worry, you can quit right here." Those are the days to utilize the examples given above to make sure that your discipline doesn't falter. Before you ever quit, miss a workout, stay out too late, or eat what you know is wrong for you, ask yourself, "Am I flapping my wings to move forward like a shark, or am I placing a curse of regret on myself for years to come."

CHAPTER 5

Mental Toughness

A number of years ago, a sports psychologist I worked with asked me to define mental toughness for him. Strangely enough, the concept of mental toughness seems easy to think of, but very difficult to define. I came up with a number of different thoughts on mental toughness for him, but none was a solid description. Over the past months, I have been meeting with different high level athletes and trainers, trying to better understand the problem, but no one had one clear answer.

During my time here as a trainer, I have seen many of us experiment with the concept of mental toughness on the athletes. Over this time, I have tried to develop tests and certain sessions around the concept of mental toughness to not only help the athlete to understand it, but also for me to get a better picture as well. Using this, meeting with athletes and trainers on the subject as well as reading a number of books on the subject, I have come to some general conclusions about this type of training.

Mental toughness is a personal, persevering decision. You can view this as an athlete's desire to continue exercise, even when passing through higher and higher levels of fatigue. When I began to experiment with athletes and myself with fatigue, I came to see some interesting results. I used to believe that everything about fatigue could be defined physiologically. I used to watch the athletes on the track and almost envision the physiological mechanisms that were running out to stop the athlete from performing. There are 5 physiological mechanisms of fatigue that I am concerned with. Depletion of the energy systems, inadequacy of the circulatory and respiratory systems, body temperature elevation, neurological insufficiency and dehydration can all lead to fatigue.

As I read more about these mechanisms I saw that all of them had their shortcomings. How do I then explain the marathon runner that can run 4 minute mile pace with a heart rate of 200? How do I explain the man who, at risk of death, was able to tread water for 40 hours until he was rescued? How do you watch a fighter continue for over an hour and never give in? Surely their systems would have run out. Further still, how do I explain the fact that other racers in that marathon had the same potential physiologically, but couldn't keep up? Or what about the other two treaders that could not stay above water and were lost at sea? Why does the fighter who is still fresher than his opponent just give up? There is one explanation. Mental toughness stems from the interaction of the

mind and the body.

Mental toughness can be seen as desire or willpower. I have watched athletes persevere through levels of pain that others are not willing to endure. These athletes all have a level of excellence set much higher than that of other athletes. I noticed from my conversations with elite athletes that they all had the wisdom of delayed gratification. They were all ready to pay the price hard now, for the prize that might even rest years from now. The interesting part was that the prize was very different for all the athletes. I think it is very important for the athlete to know themselves and to know what it is they are really after.

I asked a top level track and field athlete how he could be ranked top 10 in the world for the last 6 years, but could never crack the top five. His answer was interesting. He believed he had the talent and the skill to be number one in the world, but at that moment whenever it was time, mentally, there was something missing. He felt that

during his upbringing in this country that his mom would console him too much. For instance, she would bake a cake when things didn't go well and show him everything would be alright. The top athlete in his event for the last 8 years, he contended, was from a brutally tough country in which you fought for everything you ever had. This was the mental edge he had all his life that made the difference.

I spoke with a nationally recognized speaker at length about the topic of mental training and he also had an interesting story to add. When he was a child he was being chased by a big dog in the neighborhood. When he got to his house, there were 8 steps that he had to clear to get inside safe. He said without even thinking he hit the bottom step perfectly and made the jump. He thought about this even up to the present day 40 years later and didn't think he could have ever made that leap again. He believed that it is a sense of necessity that drives the athlete to superperformance. Something inside the athlete, whether it is his need to win, his life is at stake, money, or the applause of the crowd, the necessity is there. This is what the athlete must decide for himself and believe in. Without some need, the athlete eventually will not succeed at the highest level.

Interesting studies have been performed on sedentary and professional athletes and their ability to withstand exertion. Sedentary people always gave up early, with no signs of really approaching any true fatigue. The professional athletes, on the other hand, were able to withstand huge amounts of work and continue to go on. This tells me that mental toughness is learned and it can be trained just like any other skill. To get to a higher level you must continually push the envelope of your own limits. The best athletes have a great ability to do this. Jerry Rice, one of the best receivers in the NFL is a great example of this. In his training, Jerry runs up a mountain every morning before he starts

his training for the day. Other athletes from the NFL would come and try to train with Jerry because he was the best in the league. Upon trying to run the mountain, none of the athletes could make it and they would invariably go home because they could not compete. What was a regular day for Jerry, other athletes were not prepared for. His level of toughness was so much higher, it can be said this is a big factor in his success as a pro athlete.

Now, you might be saying, "Where is he going with this stuff?" Hopefully, you have a much better idea of the mental aspects of training as well as learn to better understand something about yourself. Now you must see that beside the training you have been doing so far in your sessions, there has to be a portion that focuses on the mental development as an athlete. There is something to be said about a "brutally hard" session, but athletes must be shown the value of what they are learning from it. An athlete working so hard he is "puking" is not good. An athlete being shown the value of learning how to go to the next level in the training, and knowing that he may become a better athlete from it may respond more positively.

Different bits of advice can be given to the kids in different ways. Test yourself in drills and examine the value of what you have accomplished. Do not become a self fulfilling prophecy with words like "I can't" during the last few minutes of the session. You can even begin the session with the message to yourself that you are going to be here for one hour. That hour is a gift. You can do the most with it or squander it, and the hour will still eventually be over. What happens during that hour is the accomplishment or the let down. Get yourself to believe that a little on top of a little eventually becomes a lot. Finally, I will leave you with a quote from a poster I hung in my room when I was in

college. The poster is of the great Russian Greco-Roman wrestler Alexander Karelin. He is throwing a huge 300 pound man in the air, and the quote below him reads, "I train harder everyday of my life than you will ever train one day in your life." This is the epitome of mental toughness training.

CHAPTER 6

The Lessons of Losing

A positive reaction to losing is essential for an athlete to reach true greatness. Losing in athletics can also be synonymous with failure. Losing or failure is the means for the growth of an athlete in a variety of ways. Losing is a natural process that must occur at all levels of athletics. There is no athlete that I have ever heard of that did not lose at some time in their career. To go even further, I cannot really think of any great athlete that did not have to come back from the adversity of loss on at least one occasion. How that particular athlete deals with loss is what is truly important. Without proper understanding of what occurred, there will be no such growth. This chapter is designed to demonstrate the reality of loss to the athlete, and assist the athlete in athletic and personal progress.

Look at how most athletic events are designed. There is usually going to be one winner, and in many cases, numerous losers (even second place is the first loser). We as athletes find many ways to rationalize loss through a variety of reasons. We let a certain placing stand out as a victory to us, such as coming in second in a field of 30 still isn't so bad, right? We also often find ways to take the blame off of ourselves such as blaming a loss on a teammate or coach. Many of us will look at the judges or rules and determine that they were unfair. Some of us will state they weren't really prepared, so the loss wasn't their fault. Finally, many athletes feel better after slandering their opponents in an attempt to make them appear less victorious. These are all normal rationales that we as athletes and humans perform. The problem here lies that instead of really identifying the

causes of the loss, we avoid it, and therefore, never grow from it. Without this growth, true mastery of the event will never occur.

There are many ways to grow from loss. The first is to accept that the loss occurred, and that you did have something to do with it. After this, the athlete must uncover what were the critical errors that happened that contributed to the loss. This could have been lack of principle centered training, poor diet, a technical flaw during the event, a loss of concentration, or even a poorly formed strategy or plan. There is an unlimited number of reasons why the loss could have occurred. The most difficult step for the athlete is to be critical of one's own performance and how it could have been improved. This is an important place where growth as an athlete and person occur. Interestingly, I have noticed over the years that the best athletes in their respective events have a great ability to do this. They are also usually the athletes that fail in some way on a consistent basis and grow from their failures. After a loss, they are calmer, and can tell you exactly the reasons why the loss occurred. There are no excuses, just explanations.

I believe that becoming critical of one's own performance is a skill just as difficult to learn as any other athletic technique. Many athletes find it difficult to accept criticism, especially if they have to give it to themselves. No one wants to feel that they are not as good as they wish they were. No one likes to admit when they have made a mistake. I will assert again, however, that the best athletes have the ability to do this whether they like it or not. Becoming more critical of one's own training lifestyle and performance will lead to certain growth and improvement. The awareness is what empowers the athlete to change. Without this awareness, the athlete stagnates and remains at the same level. By understanding this, not only should the athlete that aspires

to greatness accept loss, but he should then welcome it as an opportunity to learn and grow afterwards. If the athlete can do this, then not only is the loss less traumatic, it causes immediate stimulus for change for the better.

I often ask athletes why they are training with me or training at all. Many say they want to make the team. Many say they want to be a better player. Many say they want to continue as far as possible in athletics. Many say they want to get into better condition. When I ask , "So why is this important?", they start to run out of answers. Some say they feel if they were a better player they would win more or get into a good school. Some believe that training will make them more popular. When I ask, "So why is that important?", they usually don't have any more answers. I then ask, "How would you feel if you were a better player? How would you feel if you were in the shape of your life and got into the school of your dreams? How would you feel if you were more popular and a big reason for your team's success?" Every time the answer is the same. "I would feel great!"

That is the important piece that I think everyone forgets about athletics and training. Everything we do is to feel great about ourselves. As humans, we either do things to feel great or to avoid feeling bad. Understanding this important concept will help the athlete to deal better with loss. Do not rationalize the result to avoid feeling bad, but realize that what we aspire to is to have our dreams come true athletically so that we feel great. When we really see this, then we will see losing as a chance to get closer to feeling great, and improvement as an athlete and a person. So knowing why we really do everything that we do should make it easier when training is hard, losses have occurred, or we are feeling down. Without this knowledge, it is easier to give up or stay at the same

level. A great athlete once told me that even when times were tough and the situation looked bleak, "There is no other place I would rather be, because this is what I love to do and it makes me feel good." Another great coach of mine once told me that if you are not failing a lot of times per day, you are not taking enough chances to grow.

Loss can be a devastating event for athletes, especially at a higher level. Not only are they less often used to experiencing loss, but also loss can really affect their career, longevity, and financial status. No where is that more apparent than in non team sports like boxing, tennis, wrestling, skiing, surfing, and many other Olympic and non-Olympic sports that involve single competitors. Here there is no luxury of having a team to fall back on. Oftentimes, the athletes have trained long and hard for a single event in which they know there can only be one winner. There is no where more important for an athlete to use the techniques described above than here. Growth is essential for the non-team sportsman. Without it, they will never ascend to the higher ranks. I have seen many athletes become depressed following a loss. Whenever this occurs, I always leave them with this quote to think about by Theodore Roosevelt. "It is not the critic that counts… The credit belongs to the man in the arena, who strives violently, who errs and comes up short again and again…Who if he wins, knows the triumph of high achievement, but who if he fails, fails while daring greatly." Failure while daring greatly sounds so much better than losing. I think athletes need to perceive this and understand how important it is who they are and why they risk what they do. I have been told that the road to greatness is always under construction. I believe that losses are a foundation on which that greatness is built.

Finally, I will leave you with a list I have carried in my wallet for almost fifteen years. I found the card on the floor of the Furman University library one night studying. This card has reminded me of many important truths about winning and losing every time I consult it. It was compiled by a man named Sydney J. Harris whom I know nothing about.

How to Tell a Winner from a Loser

1. A winner says, "let's find out"; A loser says, "nobody knows."
2. When a winner makes a mistake, he says, "I was wrong"; When a loser makes a mistake, he says, "it wasn't my fault."
3. A winner goes through a problem, a loser goes around it and never gets past it.
4. A winner makes commitments and a loser makes promises.
5. A winner says, "I'm good, but not as good as I ought to be"; a loser says, "I'm not as bad as a lot of other people."
6. A winner tries to learn from those that are superior to him; a loser tries to tear down those that are superior to him.
7. A winner says. "There ought to be a better way to do it"; a loser says, "That is the way it has always been done."

Read these over and try to see when you were guilty of being a loser. If you find them and correct them for the future, growth and improvement are sure to occur.

CHAPTER 7

The True Principles of Training

Over the last chapters I attempted to change the way readers think about their concept of training. Hopefully, the impetus to change has brought you back to read in a more open minded fashion. Remember that no one can teach you anything. As the ancient saying concludes, "When the student is ready, the teacher appears." I am just a guide to the truth, but it is you that decides to listen and are, therefore, your only teacher.

When I write about the truth, I am trying to describe what I have found over the years that which cannot be denied about training. There are many myths and fallacies about training that are passed down from athlete to athlete that are never founded in what is really true. Over the years I have read hundreds of texts by a myriad of authors in search of training methods that are really what they say they are. I don't write this to impress you, but to impress upon you the importance of challenging everything that you have done in your training in the past and ask the simple questions: What? Why? How? When? If you can answer these questions about the different aspects of your training, you will be doing well. You must back your answers with solid science and proof, not on the word of a friend that has only been lifting one week longer than you.

To help to design your training so that you minimize mistakes, I have compiled a list of training principles that you must follow to ensure proper training programs. If you violate even one of these principles, your program will have weaknesses. Violate more than one, and there will be some serious holes in your training. After reading this list, I also challenge you to examine how you have violated these principles in the past and how you could have changed the training for the better. You may kick yourself now, but it is

better late than never to start realizing your mistakes. That is the only way an athlete can grow and make progress.

The 11 Principles of Training

1. **The Principle of Understanding**

This principle represents the idea that an athlete must understand the rationale behind his or her training to get the best results. Now this does not mean that the athlete has to know the complex science behind the training, but he must have good working knowledge of what he is doing. This will allow the athlete to better believe in his trainer and training system which can only enhance the results.

2. **The Principle of Individualization**

You are unlike any other athlete in the world. What works best for someone else may not work best for you. Why then, do we try to train just like everyone else? The athlete must be evaluated for specific strengths and weaknesses and the program must focus on these areas. The training for any athlete must be specific if the athlete is ever to reach his or her full potential.

3. **The Solid Foundation Principle**

The athlete must first build a solid foundation of general physical qualities before the specific work is done. (These include speed, strength, flexibility, coordination, balance, and endurance) The more solid the foundation that is developed, the more solid the athlete can eventually become.

4. **The Principle of Specialization**

To ever fully reach his or her potential, the athlete must eventually focus on a single sport or discipline. The athlete should not strive to be a "jack of all trades," but a "master of one." This specialization can not occur until the solid foundation is in place.

5. **The Principle of Periodization**

Periodization can simply be defined as having a plan. A coach once told me that "failing to plan is planning to fail." As when following the previous principles, the plan must be known, individualized, and built with a solid foundation. There are many ways to go about the plan which will be discussed in its own respected chapter.

6. **The Principle of Training Economy**

Once he or she has begun their plan, the athlete must choose exercises and methods which utilize training economy. This means selecting an exercise that gives you the highest returns from your training in the least amount of time. This takes experience and knowledge, but over the course of this book, you will be better armed to select those exercises.

7. **The Principle of Continuity**

Now that the plan has been stated, it is imperative that the athlete works continuously toward this goal. It is always easy to start something, but very difficult for many to carry it through. If one wants to achieve true success or reach his or her potential, there cannot be long breaks from training.

8. **The Principle of Progressive Overload**

Now the plan has been stated and the athlete is continuously training. What if the athlete does the same workouts for a year? How long will it take until he stops progressing? This is why loads must change to allow for continued physiological and psychological changes. How and when to do this is covered in this text.

9. **The Principle of Variety**

Now even though an athlete can increase the loads, no athlete can increase the loads forever. If this were so, we would all be lifting over 1000 pounds on every lift. So besides changing the loads, the stimulus must also be changed to ensure progression and avoid boredom and overtraining. When to change the lifts and how to recognize the time for change will also be explained later.

10. **The Principle of Proper Nutrition**

Athletes must follow a proper diet in order to progress in training. If there is not the right "fuel in the tank" the athlete will not run properly, nor will his body have the building blocks to grow and recover from workouts. I know it is going to take some time to change the readers view on diet, but I am going to do my best.

11. **The Principle Recovery and Restoration**

The athlete must always adhere to the proper amount of rest and recovery in order for the body to supercompensate to the stimuli. One must remember that real progress does not occur when you are working out, it occurs when you are recovering after that workout.

Make sure you can support all of these principles in your training and you will be on the right track. Soon I will cover each one in depth to allow you to help design your ultimate training program.

CHAPTER 8

The Principle of Understanding

In the previous chapter, I listed the 11 principles of training that must be adhered to in order to ensure optimal results. Over the next number of chapters I am going to explain each principle more in depth and give readers insight into how to maximize their training for any sport. The first principle of training dictates that athletes must have an understanding of their training. Without a working understanding, it will truly be impossible for athletes to *believe* in their training. To really exemplify this point, I would like to tell a story I heard years ago from my mentor, Bill Parisi.

There once was a tightrope walker named Philipe. He was regarded as the best tightrope walker in all of Europe because he had developed a new style of tightrope walking. What he used instead of a long pole for balance was a special wheelbarrow filled with 100 kilos of stones. Philipe was not satisfied with being considered the best walker in Europe, he wanted to be the best in the world. To achieve this, he knew he had to do something spectacular. He came to the United States and Canada and asked permission to walk across the Niagra Falls with his wheelbarrow. He was granted the use of the falls and on the day of the walk, many spectators, reporters and crews from around the world were there. As he began his walk, he slowly walked his wheelbarrow out over the falls. As he approached the middle, he began to slow down and teeter from side to side. Mothers covered their children's eyes and the crowd gasped. He regained control and slowly proceeded across the falls. After several minutes, he made it within ten feet of the end. At this point, he pushed the wheelbarrow across to the end and stood alone on the cable. He pulled out a blindfold, blindfolded himself and then did 2 cartwheels to the

other side to safety. The crowd erupted when they saw he was in control the entire time. The crowd swarmed him and the flashbulbs ignited. Later, after many of the crowd had left, Philipe walked up to a reporter and asked if he could ask *him* a question. The reporter was confused and said yes. Philipe said, "Do you think I can take my wheelbarrow and walk back across the falls?" The reporter was stunned, thought for a moment and said, "Well, yes, Philipe I saw you do it, I think you can." Then Philipe asked another question. He inquired, "Do you believe I can take my wheelbarrow and walk back across the falls?" Now the reporter was confused. "Do I believe you can? Well, yes I already said that, yes I believe you can." Philipe smiled and said, "Then come with me." The two walked over to the ledge with the wheelbarrow and Philipe dumped out the 100 kilos of stone. He said, "If you believe I can do it, *get in the wheelbarrow.*"

This story has a powerful message. Until you really believe in something, you will never achieve the results you could. I feel that to truly believe in anything, you must understand it as much as possible. Look at great athletes in many different sports. If you were to ask them about rules, strategy, tactics, or techniques in their sport, they could probably explain them with great detail. They understand these things and they believe in them. Now ask that same athlete about the proper ways to train. You will hear many different ideas without much good scientific explanation. You will also probably hear how they have tried many different methods of training because they could not find one they truly believed in. This switching around from training to training, trainer to trainer, never allows for confidence or performance to grow to its potential.

I am not saying that an athlete has to know training down to the deepest scientific foundations, but he must have good working knowledge of what is going on. To help simplify this for the athlete, I have developed a simple system of 4 questions an athlete must ask of his training program. These questions are *What, How, Why and When*? If the athlete can answer these questions about his training with better working knowledge, it will be easier to believe in and produce results from his training.

First, the athlete must ask: **What?** Good questions are as follows: What is the exercise that they are performing? What are the main muscles that it works? What is the correct resistance? What is the correct number of reps and sets? What is the correct tempo and rest period? What is the best way to warm up for the exercise? What should be the order of the exercise?

Second, the athlete must ask: **How?** How is the exercise best performed? How can I change the exercise to achieve different results? How is this exercise specific to what I am trying to achieve? How is this exercise going to help me improve? How long do I perform this exercise for before I change?

Third, the athlete must ask: **Why?** Why is this exercise a good choice? Why is this exercise going to help me achieve my goals? Why should the exercise be performed only a certain way?

Finally, the fourth question is: **When?** When is the best time to use this exercise? When in the training cycle should this exercise be added? When do I stop using a certain exercise if results are declining?

I think that questions facilitate the growth of an athlete, both mentally and physically. I instruct my athletes to question everything. There is so much mythology

out there about training that too often we subscribe to methods that we do not *understand or believe*. Without the questioning process, there would never be any improvement. There is always a better way. This book was written to give you the tools to find it.

CHAPTER 9

The Principle of Individualization

Every principle that will be described from this point will build upon the principles that proceed it. This means that in order to follow the Principle of Individualization, one must first have an understanding of what it means to be an individual as an athlete. To many, this may sound like common sense, but I assure you that most athletes do not find what individually works for them. Think back to most of the training you have performed in your life. Did you create it with your specific abilities and goals in mind? Did you just read the program in a magazine or book? Did a friend or training partner show you the program and you both proceeded to perform the same exact thing? In most cases, the answer is "no" to the first question and "yes" to the second and third. If this is true, this next installment in the Principles of Training is going to help you to break old habits and release untapped potential.

As with the last principle, I believe a story is a powerful way to hammer home the truth. I once met an outstanding American wrestler that came to hear me speak on wrestling training. His coaches were in attendance as well, and they later offered insight into the story I am about to tell you now. This athlete was a state and national champion in high school and was considered one of the top recruits for colleges in the country. One of his greatest strengths was his explosiveness and quickness for his size. Many coaches marveled at his speed and ability to shoot for incredibly fast takedowns. After a difficult decision, the athlete chose what is considered one of the top wrestling colleges in the United States. Unfortunately, this is where the story begins to take a turn for the worse.

At this school, the athletes were worked hard and long. This training was done by all athletes on the team regardless of weight, strengths or weaknesses. For example, the athletes would run entire stadium steps for hours and perform many lifts with one set to failure. This athlete worked as hard as any, but his body and spirit began to break down. He tried to work even harder and ended up with surgery. To make the story short, the athlete never reached his potential, and lack of individualization was to blame. His coaches also stated this fact, and it is sad that it took until that day for them to finally figure out what had caused the tragedy.

How could this happen, you say? There are a few possibilities. First, the United States has millions of athletes, so someone, regardless of training is going to rise to the top. Along this path, many more talented athletes may fall by the wayside injured and ruined, but we only see the victor. These coaches and schools have a constant supply of these athletes, so they will just find someone else. Another possibility is that coaches and athletes may not be familiar with the ways to assess individual strengths and weaknesses, not to mention how to then train them. Without this ability, the coaches do what has always been done for the sake of hard work instead of smart work.

What I call for is a "nurturing" process for the individual athlete. With proper testing and evaluation of the results, athletes can better identify their strengths and weaknesses, select the right training stimuli for their particular goals, and ultimately help to decide what sport they are best suited for. This process has gone on for a number of years in the former Soviet Union and China where children were tested and selected as athletes and then developed individually into world champions. Now I am not saying we

need to go to this level, but a better understanding of what makes an individual tick has a huge impact on sport selection, training and success.

Now that we understand that an individual program is a necessity for success, I will try to help you to understand how to assess an individual. I will give sample questions that you can ask about yourself or athletes you coach that will help to assist in developing an individual program. **Is the athlete a beginner or advanced?** You would be surprised how many athletes literally have no experience and are asked to perform high level exercises and training levels. This is very common in the U.S. with our younger athletes. Just make sure the athlete has the proper base for training and is well rounded in basic biomotor abilities (speed, strength, flexibility, balance, and coordination) before pushing too far. One should also understand that the tolerance level is very different between experienced and beginner athletes. Just like a medical prescription, a training prescription should be specific and used with caution. **What are the distinct physical traits of you or your athletes?** This is where one should have no problem understanding that we all are different and have different training needs. Does the short athlete train the same way as the tall one? Does the fatter athlete run as far as the leaner one? Of course not, but we see it in every sport, don't we. The athlete and coach must begin to understand what these differences mean and how to work with them, not against them. **What are the strengths and weaknesses of you or your athlete?** As I said earlier, the coach or athlete must first learn to assess and interpret these, and then the athlete must work on both. I have seen too many athletes only work on their strengths and further ignore their weaknesses. This will eventually come back to haunt the athlete. I always say that a good athlete works only on what he is good at, a great athlete works

on what he is not good at, masters it and becomes a champion. **What are the specific needs of the athlete's sport?** All too often, I have watched athletes try to perform training routines of their favorite athlete even though they are involved in a different sport. The coach and athlete must take into account the specific demands of their sport and design the program accordingly to the individual. **Where is the athlete in terms of training plan?** Many athletes do not vary their training as a season or match approaches. Others follow along with changes a training partner is making even though it is not time for them to do so. The athlete must learn his or her own individual needs for training variety as an important event approaches. **Is the athlete a male or a woman?** Another common mistake I often see is coaches or athletes trying to train female athletes just like the males. There are differences in musculature, bone structure and hormones that dictate that this should not happen. Understanding the training differences between the two is crucial to ensuring that both reach their ultimate potential.

Hopefully, these questions have stimulated you to further question your own training programs and needs. No one athlete is exactly the same as another. No athlete responds the same to different stimuli as another. These facts alone should have you asking the question every time you train: How is this suited best to my individual strengths, weaknesses, and need? As they say in the United States, you must first always look out for number one... If you don't, you might just step in number two.

CHAPTER 10

The Principle of a Solid Foundation

The foundation of an athlete's ability has a huge impact on their chances for success in sport. If the foundation is deficient in certain parameters or incompletely developed, performance is sure to suffer.

One of the crucial tasks of a great trainer is to first identify the necessary criteria required for successful performance in high level sport, and then whether the athlete is lacking in any of these areas. After the deficiencies have been found, the trainer must use the proper methods to reverse the missing links in the chain.

I have found an interesting trend among all athletes over my years of training. Most athletes do have an idea of their particular strengths and weaknesses when it relates to their chosen sport. All you have to do is ask the elite athlete about his or her deficiencies and they usually have no trouble explaining them to you in depth. What I find so interesting is that athletes will always work more on their strengths when they are left to their own training. For instance, when an athlete that has great strength, but lacks flexibility and speed is left to train on his own, he will usually opt for more strength work even though he knows what he is missing. Because of this, I have developed a saying that I use with my younger athletes very often: "A good athlete works on what he is good at. A great athlete works on what he is not good at, until he makes even his weaknesses his strengths." This may sound like a simple concept, but ask yourself how many times you really focused on your weaknesses when you could work on your strengths instead. I know I have been guilty of doing this many times.

This concept can best be illustrated with a story I heard long ago that I tell to all of my athletes. The story is one of my all-time favorites. There was once a boy that was

born with only his right arm. The left arm was missing all the way to the shoulder. As he grew into his teens and began to attend high school, he was always treated differently by the students. Not that they treated him badly, but he felt that he never got their respect as a full human being. Every day his mother would drive him home from school, and on the way they would always pass a judo academy. He begged his mother every time to try the academy, and she would always say no, fearing the one armed boy would easily get injured. All of his nagging eventually paid off, however, and they went to the academy. The academy was run by an older Japanese master that instantly took to the boy. As soon as he saw him and his limitation, he instructed the boy to come 3 times per week and that he would personally train him in the art of judo. Three times per week the boy would attend and each time the boy and master worked on counters, but only one throw.

After the first six months of training, the boy began to question this training and asked his master, "Master, why am I only working on one move, when the other students are working on many?" The master replied that this was a difficult move to learn and that he had to continue to practice it. Six more months of training went by and the one-armed boy became very frustrated, and thought about quitting. When he went to tell his master he was frustrated, the master replied, "Good, I have entered you in the State Tournament this weekend. This will be a good test for your training." At this point the boy was terrified. He did not tell his parents or any of his friends for fear of embarrassment.

That weekend the boy and his master attended the tournament and the master's only instructions were to use the counters and one throw that he had learned. As the boy walked to the center of the mat during the first round, the crowd was suspicious of what

they would see. The boy and his opponent tangled, he countered the opponent and landed a hard throw for full ippon (this is a throw in which the opponent lands flat on their back and the match is ended). The boy had won his first match and the crowd was stunned! In the second round, the boy again countered and landed the full point ippon throw again. The crowd was now following the boy during the tournament. In round three, the boy met a tougher opponent, but the result was the same; he landed his only throw for ippon. Now the crowd was cheering him on! The boy had made it to the finals against the 3-time champion. This would be no easy match, and the opponent would not go easy on the boy, one-armed or not. The boy was scared, but the master instructed him in the same way as before. The match began and the stronger opponent was manhandling the boy, but he was countering well. The boy was getting pushed around, but not giving any ground. Finally, in an explosive movement, the boy masterfully attacked and landed his only throw for full point and the win. The crowd exploded and carried the boy out of the arena on their shoulders. On the ride home, the boy, after he had celebrated, asked the master if this was a set up or some kind of trick. The master answered, "Son, you mastered a very difficult throw." The boy heard this, but still didn't believe him. Then the master stopped the car, looked into the boy's eyes and told him the secret, "Son, the only counter to your one throw is for your opponent to grab and control your **LEFT** arm." The master had made the boy's greatest weakness his greatest strength.

Now I know what you are saying, "Well how am I supposed to know where my strengths and weaknesses lie?" That can be illustrated in a number of ways. First, if you have the luxury of an advanced sports trainer, they should be able to perform an extensive evaluation that involves speed, strength, power, flexibility, diet, coordination, balance,

agility, endurance, mental toughness, and skill. Since most do not have this luxury, I have created a method for you to assess yourselves, and then it is up to you to hold yourself to the results. This self assessment tool is described in the next paragraph, and pictured at the end of this chapter.

First you must draw two circles, each on a separate piece of paper. The first will be called the elite athlete wheel, and the second will be your personal athletic assessment wheel. After you have drawn them, I want you to add 8 even spokes to this wheel. The eight spokes will then be individually labeled for upper body strength, lower body strength, core strength, speed, endurance, flexibility, diet, and technique. After you have labeled each spoke I want you to make ten small lines on each spoke to signify levels 1-10 for each ability on each spoke. This has been done on the flexibility spoke on the enclosed wheel example. The number one will be closest to the center of the wheel and the number ten will be the rim of the wheel. After you have done this on both circles, they are ready to be used. First, I want you to fill out the elite wheel. This is done by first picturing the abilities of the highest level people in your sport. Once you have determined these, mark them from 1-10 on the corresponding spokes for each ability. For instance, if you are a soccer player and you believe an elite soccer player must have endurance of 8, place a dot on the eighth line on that spoke. After you have done this for each ability, then you just connect the dots and fill in the area of the shape within the circle that you have made. The shaded area shows you what the elite athlete in your sport must possess to be successful. Now, fill in your circle, and be honest! After you have the two completed, compare them, and view where your weaknesses lie. You can also see where your strengths are located and better understand what type of athlete you really

are. At that point the direction of your training is up to you . Only work your strengths, and you will be limited. Work on your complete foundation, and you will rise above your competition. A wise coach once told me, “The road to success is always under construction, now get to work!”

Personal Athletic Assessment Wheel

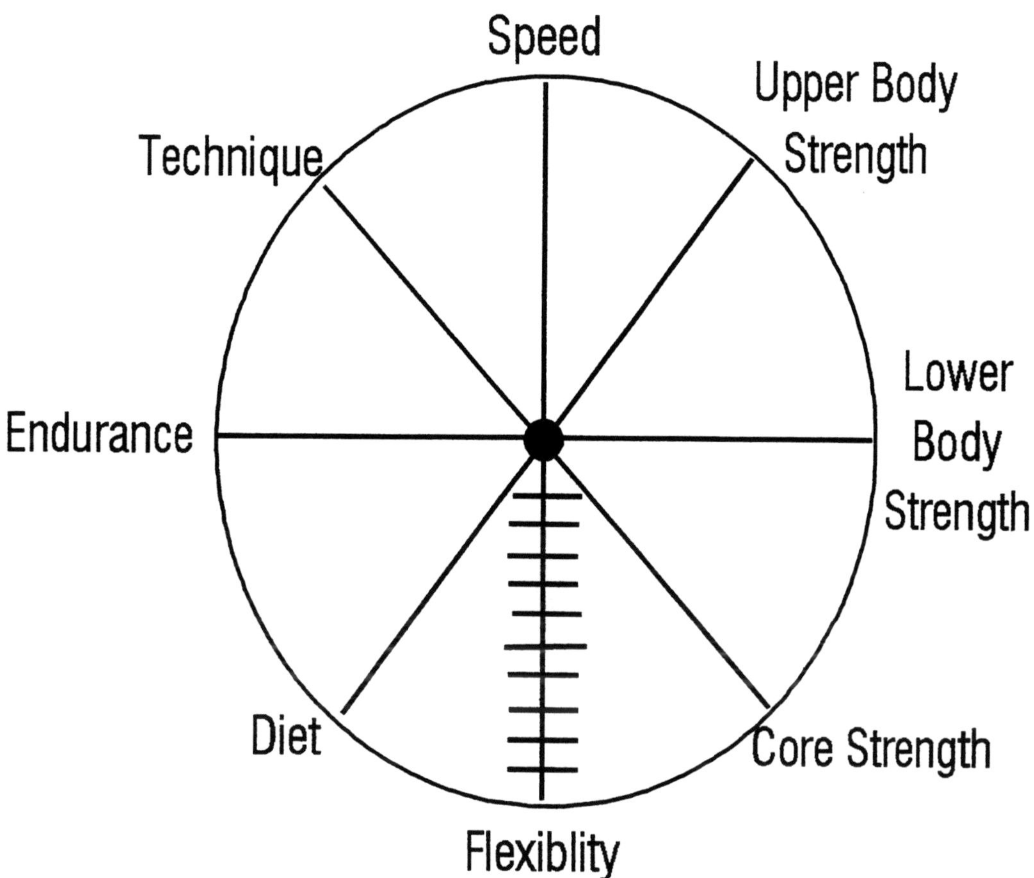

CHAPTER 11

The Principle of Specialization

I recently went to Las Vegas, and during my stay, I had a chance to see one of the popular shows there. There were many animals in the show, but the lions were the most impressive. They were huge, strong and intimidating when compared to the size of their trainer. The show had all the lights, glitter and technology one would expect to see in Vegas, yet one thing had me confused. The trainer still used a chair to tame the lions when they got restless. I thought to myself, "With all that money at his disposal, the trainer is still only using the chair to tame the lions?" Surely something must be better and safer. But it was later explained to me that the chair is still the most powerful tool when used correctly. By pointing the four legs of the chair at the lion, he will try to keep his eye on each leg at one time. This divides his attention, and keeps him under total control. When your attention is split in to many directions, it will always hold you back from your main goals. I see this in athletics every day.

In previous chapters, I have described the principles in a sort of order. I want you to understand that specialization cannot occur until you know which direction you should go (Principle of Conscious Involvement) and have developed the optimal athletic base (Principle of a Solid Foundation) for your individual strengths and weaknesses (Principle of Individuality). Once this has occurred, you should already be headed in the right direction of your athletic specialization.

Early Specialization in Sport

There are a number of athletes today that are gaining incredible success due to their early specialization in sport. No one is a better example of this than the golfer,

Tiger Woods. Tiger's father was a golf caddie and coach and taught Tiger to swing like a pro by the time he was three. In fact, it is well known that Tiger beat his first pro golfer before he was 5 years old! By 17, he was and still is considered the best golfer on the planet. He did more than specialize, he devoted himself entirely to his sport. Even though this type of early specialization is uncommon, there is an explanation on why this occurred.

Just like a child learning several languages or a prodigy learning music, science has found that there are optimal times in a human's life to do certain things. When you miss these developmental stages, one will find it hard to ever catch up. This is due to something called neural plasticity. This means that the brain and nervous system have certain best times to allow for abilities to be developed. For instance, learning a language, from the sounds and intonations you make, to processing what the words mean is best done before the age of 10. Have you ever listened to a person when they tried to learn a new language at 18 or over? They always have a weird accent and can't get the words right. This is because the neural plasticity is gone and they missed the best time to develop that skill. Now imagine if Tiger picked up golf at 18, the results would be similar to learning a new language. His swing would be less smooth, and his touch would probably be average at best. This should demonstrate to you that to be successful in your sport goals, there must be the right amount of focus on the right things at the right times.

The Eastern European Countries have spent many years training and studying the training of athletes. Much of what I practice today is a result of their athletic research. These countries with relatively small populations were able to produce as many elite

athletes as much larger competing countries. This was due to the fact that they knew how and when to specialize. Most of their literature asserts that an athlete must begin to specialize toward their sport by about 13-14 years of age. This is, of course, after developing a great base and education of training has occurred. This way, the coaches were able to pick what sport the athlete was best suited for according to their abilities. After they were selected for their best sport, then there was time to make them into a world champion.

The Ability to Focus

An athlete that cannot truly focus can never truly specialize. Many of the athletes that come to train with me have never learned how to focus. They may have great skill or physical abilities, but almost all of the athletes never know how to focus the best way that they can. When I work with my athletes, I first define focus for them. I believe that focus is a combination of an athlete's priorities and that athlete's actions. Most athletes I work with have one of the two components of focus, but rarely do they ever have the two aligned properly. Many athletes know their priorities, they just usually don't do the right things to carry them out. Some athletes also do a lot of training, but it is for the wrong reason. I want to share an example of both of these situations. Then you can understand the consequences of what happens when you are missing either side of your focus.

An illustration of having the right priorities but the wrong actions can be seen through a female athlete I am working with. Her name is Adrienne Johnson and she plays in the WNBA for the Orlando Miracle. Adrienne is coming back from an Achilles tendon tear that happened during the previous season. When she came to me, her

priorities were to get stronger, faster and to improve her diet. These were directly aligned with getting her back to the top of her game. The problem was that she was only playing basketball and jogging on the treadmill a few times per week to address these priorities. So one can see that she had her priorities set in a good order; she just was not taking the right action toward them. Though an outsider may have viewed her as focused, now you can see she was only half way there. Once I created her training program of sprinting, lifting and diet that aligned with her priorities, then her focus became complete. Now she feels she is in better condition than before the injury and is prepared to break the three-point record she is on pace for this season.

The second example of improper focus is when you have good actions, but your priorities are wrong. This is a difficult parable I am about to tell, because the lesson is aimed at a good friend. Flavio Almeida is 4-time National champion and 2-time world champion in jiu jitsu. Whenever we are together, I am always trying to push him further as an athlete both physically and mentally. When I challenged him about his priorities, he stated that his main priority was to win the Worlds this June. Anyone who knows Flavio would say he is incredibly dedicated, but I am about to show that even dedicated athletes can improve their focus. Flavio separated his shoulder badly while snowboarding in Vermont the last time he was there, and the shoulder is not healing well. This injury is an incredible setback both physically and mentally. I wanted him to stay and train instead of going on that trip so we could get ready for the Worlds. When I reminded him about this after the injury, he answered that he can't abstain from all "fun" things. This is the priority dilemma. Was the main priority the Worlds or was it fun? If both sides of the focus were aligned, I assure you the injury would never have happened.

Picture the chair and the lion example again. By looking at too many legs (snowboarding, fun, jiu jitsu), the focus is divided and the lion paralyzed (injury). The moral is to always ask yourself if your priorities are correct and what you are doing to directly address them.

CHAPTER 12

The Principle of Periodization

The concept of periodization, having a plan, is the reason why I was given the opportunity to write for *Gracie Magazine*. When I was first introduced to Luca Atalla, the magazine's editor, he wasted no time in picking my brain about many different aspects of training. Most of those questions revolved around the concept of periodization. At the time, Luca was doing what most people do when they are working out. He was following a workout program from a book that he had heard was very good. Now looking back on the book and the workout, he found that they violated just about every principle we have discussed up to this point. For instance, the program was not well defined for jiu jitsu, so it was difficult to develop conscious involvement and believe in the program. The program was also the same for everyone that followed it, so there was no individuality. The program had no concern for the level you were at, so a solid foundation was not a prerequisite to start. The workout lacked focus as well, so I believe specialization would also be impossible. The interesting thing about that book that makes it appealing to an athlete is that the training was periodized. There was a plan. Unfortunately, as I will show you, if you violate all the other principles, periodization by itself means nothing.

There are many books written on the concept of periodization, and as a result, one may think it is difficult to understand. The concept is quite simple, it is the use of the concept where the art of training comes in. Everything in life can be broken down into periods. Whether we are looking at hours, days, months, or years, they are all nothing but periods of time. Periodization is nothing more than cycling training during periods of time in order to achieve a goal. When you really look at it, periodization is just a fancy

way of forming a training plan to get a certain result. Let me use some examples of when periodization can lead to no results or even a drop off in performance. The easiest way to see periodization used in these wrong ways is to go to your local gym on the same day of the week for a few weeks in a row. The odds are that you will see the same people doing the exact same workout with the exact same weight and repetitions. Yes, they are working out, but without a goal and a plan to attain it, you are going to stay right where you are. Be honest, how many of you have done the same lifts on the same days of the week for years, or know an athlete that has? I'm sure every one of you will raise your hand. The other example is to find the athlete that is always pushing his limits every time he or she works out. The odds are for this athlete that he will become injured or develop an overuse syndrome in the areas they like to work the most. I know every one of you can also think of a few injured athletes right now that are a result of not cycling their training correctly. So you see, both examples of athletes probably did not specify their goal well enough and never really developed a good plan to attain it.

Setting goals in training is the first and most crucial part in the Principle of Periodization. Without them, you are never really going anywhere. Goals must have three important characteristics. The goals must be realistic, measurable and have a time frame attached to them. If any one of these is missing, you will not be able to periodize your training properly. When a goal is realistic, it means that you can attain that goal. For instance, if you are a blue belt in jiu jitsu and you want to become a black belt in one year, this is not a realistic goal. Because it is unrealistic, you would be unable to create the proper training to get there. For a goal to be measurable, you must add measurements or values to parameters in your training so you can constantly assess progress. For

instance, your measurable goal cannot be, " I want to run the 100 meter faster." It must be, "I will run the 100 meter in 10.81 seconds." Now the goal is exact and progress can be checked. Finally, you must attach a time period to your goal. Without a period of time to follow, periodization would be impossible to create. So the goal, "I will squat 200 kilos by June 30th" now forces the athlete to periodize the training properly to get there.

There are two great pieces of advice I can give to an athlete that wants to plan out their training effectively. The first is something I got from Steven Covey's book, The Seven Habits of Highly Effective People. Every athlete must Begin with the End in Mind. What I mean by this is that I always instruct my athletes to plan their training backward. There are so many athletes that try to build their program day by day for an event that is a year away. I think that will be almost impossible to achieve great results. If you plan your training backward, from the result you want to achieve (goal), your planning will be easier and you will be able to monitor progress about where you should always be along the way. The second task I give to athletes is to write everything down. Write out every workout including exercise, reps, sets, weights, and how you felt about all of them. According to these writings, you will be able to assess and evaluate your current program . This will make it easy for you to also look back on training and plan out future programs, as well as help you to understand what works best for you. The workout journal will also be a reminder of the goal ahead and what kind of progress you are constantly making toward it. If you are not using a workout journal right now, you are missing out. Buy one, and remember, start it from the end first and record everything.

This chapter has given you the framework to write a training plan. Unfortunately, there is still much work for you to do if you ever want to be a champion. The actual training in terms of exercise selection, reps, sets, tempo, rest, and frequency will be something for you to continue to investigate on your own. For now, use all books and magazines that offer training plans cautiously. Take the things you think are good from them, but always question everything. This way you will eventually create a plan that is right for you.

Now the workout from the book that Luca was following should look more suspicious. Yes, the book changed training over certain periods of time, but there were flaws in the system. Without knowing his specific goals and the timeframe set to them, the book was not allowing Luca to form the proper plan. My Russian coach on the bobsled team used to say, "Failing to plan is planning to fail." There is no statement in training that could be more true than this.

CHAPTER 13

The Principle of Training Economy

A number of years ago, I was given a 1903 copy of Edgar Allen Poe's, The Raven. Upon opening it for the first time, there was a quote written on the inside cover that I will never forget. "Time and tide wait for no man." That quote has stuck with me for many reasons and has become part of my personal philosophy.

Humans are always looking for a way to examine or save time. From the works of Sir Isaac Newton and Albert Einstein, to the latest, fastest way to travel or even cook our food, we are always trying to manipulate time in our favor. In a way, we are always looking for a method to be more efficient when it comes to using time. One area that I found this not to be true, however, is when we are training. Let me give you an example.

A few Ultimate Fighting Championships ago, the announcers were praising Tito Ortiz for his training regimen. This supposedly included 8 hours of training per day, 6 or 7 days per week. Everyone I questioned about this felt that to become champion, this has to be how an athlete must train. Everyone must also believe that time is not really an element to examine when it comes to training. As I tell all of my athletes, however, it is not how long and hard you work, it is how smart you work that is going to make a difference. This chapter is going to cover the Principle of Training Economy. The bad news is that you are going to most likely see errors in your training as it relates to time. The good news is that you are going to have more time after you realize that "Less is more."

The concept of Training Economy relates to achieving the most with your training in the minimum amount of time. Not only will added training beyond this point not increase performance, it will likely lead to eventual injury. You must look at Training

Economy as streamlining many aspects of training to achieve maximal results with no wasted effort. When this is done properly, you will improve performance, have more time to focus on other parts of your life, and decrease the chances of injury.

Many athletes are looking to improve technique in their particular sport or skill. Usually, this improvement in technique is to make the style more efficient so there is less wasted energy. These same athletes are notorious for then going out and overtraining with their new technique until they are either overtrained or injured. Here lies the paradox. The rest of this chapter is going to demonstrate four areas of training which athletes can apply the Principle of Training Economy to enhance performance.

How Long is Too Long

Every athlete has either trained or knows an athlete that trains for hours during one workout. You know the one, in the gym for hours, set after grueling set even when their strength has left them. You usually admire that athlete for his determination and will. I want you to now view that person as someone that is wasting his time and really doesn't know what he is doing.

After a proper warmup of about 25 minutes, science has shown that a workout should not exceed 45 minutes to an hour. There are a number of factors that support this. First, in males, testosterone (the hormone that supports growth) levels begin to dwindle after a straight hour of lifting. At the same time, cortisol (the hormone that breaks down the body) levels begin to sharply increase. This means that after you have pushed for over an hour, your body is now in a catabolic state and further training will be of no

benefit. Later, when I cover the Principle of Nutrition, I will show you how to reverse these levels.

How many of you have ever seen the physiques of a marathon runner? Usually, they are very skinny and oftentimes injured. Their long workouts cause them to be in this catabolic state, and without the proper nutrients during the workout, they begin to break down their own muscle tissue. This is not what we want to achieve.

I once heard a strength coach I admire state that if you are in the gym for over an hour, you are making friends, not training. Ask yourself this question next time you go in for another long training session.

You are not doing Nothing, You are Recovering

We all know the athletes that just have to train almost every day. These compulsive individuals usually are under the mindset that if they are not training, they are getting worse. Nothing could be more the opposite of this. I used to be one of those athletes. I felt guilty if I weren't doing anything physical every day to improve my performance. That was until I realized the wisdom that I wasn't doing nothing, I was doing the most important thing; I was recovering!

To improve from the training you have just performed, you must recover and rebuild stronger than you were before. This can only occur with a decrease in activity for certain periods during training. For instance, I have found that 4 days of training per week is the optimal number for me to achieve my best results. Any more than this, I do not recover completely and performance suffers.

Question your training and find your optimal number of days per week. I'm sure it will be less than you are using currently, and now find some productive things to do in all the free time you just gained!

All Exercises are not Created Equal

Now that you are gaining a idea of how long the workout should be, you have to fill the workout with the right economical exercises. Choosing the most economical exercises will help you to save both time and energy.

Let us look at one of the most popular exercises in the gym, the bicep curl. This can be done using the bar, dumbbells, cables, bands or just about anything that stresses the muscles. Everyone has usually done this exercise and lots of sets of it for sure. Now look at the size of the muscle compared to the rest of your body, and then ask yourself if that muscle is really that important to your sport. You will probably find that the muscle is small in relation to the rest of your physique and that it really doesn't help your sport too much at all. The funny part is that the bicep is not even the main muscle used to flex the arm and that you can tear this muscle off and not really lose too much function at all.

Let's compare the bicep curl to 2 of my favorite exercises, the pull up and the wide grip deadlift. The bicep curl works only a few muscles primarily in the forearm and arm. The pull up works almost every muscle in the upper body, and the wide grip deadlift works almost every muscle in the entire body! The bicep curl is also not too specific of a movement when it comes to sport, whereas the pull up and deadlift motions are more related to actual sport movement. So as you can see by this example, the bicep curl is not a time efficient lift and should probably be used sparingly in your training.

Decrease the Intensity, Turn Down the Volume

Now you have an understanding of the proper length of a workout and an idea about exercise selection. You must also understand that how intense and how much you do of that exercise also relates to training economy. You must always strive to perform the minimal intensity and volume to achieve the results you want.

For instance, when it comes to intensity, you must select the right amount of weight for the job. People with less training experience can perform at a much lower level and still make gains. The more advanced you are, the higher the intensity must be to still reach desired goals.

In terms of volume in training, if you could achieve the same results running 400 meters 5 times or 10 times, you must select 5 repetitions. This will save time, energy, and decrease the chance of injury. We are not here to do more just because it is tough; we are here to do the right amount for what we are trying to accomplish.

I have just helped you to shorten and decrease the number of training sessions per week. These sessions should also now be filled with the right exercises at the right intensity and volume. All of these changes in your program should now free up much more time for you. Remember that this time has to do with actual training. You can still focus plenty of time on developing your training plan, technique and nutrition. Just because you have more time on your hands does not mean you don't have to spend it wisely. Like the saying goes, "An ounce of gold cannot buy an ounce of time." Use it wisely.

CHAPTER 14

The Principle of Continuity

One of the things I like most about sports is their many different traditions. Whether it be wearing certain national or team colors, singing songs that are passed down through the generations, or eating the different foods served at different sporting events, I enjoy them all. Everyone that has been involved with sports has taken part in some tradition of that sport along the way, and usually people have a favorite. There is one tradition in American College Sport that is one of my favorites. At Clemson University, before every football game, the entire team assembles at the top of a hill which runs down the middle of the 80,000 seat stadium. As the team becomes visible at the top of the hill, the crowd gets into a frenzy of cheering. Then in an explosion of movement, the entire team sprints down the hill into the stadium to the ear piercing crowd. Before the team sprints down to the stadium, each member of the team rubs Howard's Rock. This is a special rock from Death Valley, California, that is fixed to a podium at the top of the hill. Every athlete for every game since 1967 has rubbed this rock in the hope its mystical powers will ensure a victory for the team. It is not the sprint, the crowd or even the rubbing that I like most about the tradition, it is the fact that the rock which was once rough and sharp is now completely smooth like glass. Each man over all of those years has helped in some way to contribute to the rock's smoothness. Each rub has had significance. They are all forever part of a larger thing.

Continuity is defined as an uninterrupted connection. Continuity can also be defined as persistence toward a goal over time. Calvin Coolidge once said that, "Nothing in the world can take the place of persistence." In terms of training, I strongly agree with

this statement. The Principle of Continuity, like many of the other principles I have reviewed, is commonly violated as well as misunderstood. Many of the athletes and students I have trained have found Continuity one of the hardest principles to follow. We all know the athlete or student that only trains if something is quickly approaching. Because they are often trying to catch up for lost time, the athlete finds it much harder to peak, and there is a much greater chance of injury. Everyone probably knows an athlete that tried to quickly prepare for a competition that either did not attain the result that they had hoped for or sustained an injury that held them down. This is commonly the result of discontinuous training.

When an athlete is consistent over time, small gains will eventual equal large ones. When there are interruptions in training, an athlete's progress can be halted and even move significantly backward if the interruption is long enough. By staying consistent, an athlete is always at a higher level of readiness for his or her sport. This high level of readiness allows the athlete to peak much easier and the body is less susceptible to being injured. A quote of mine that I tell my athletes to illustrate this is that "The peak of a mountain is much easier to attain when you are three quarters of the way there than if you are starting again from the bottom, no matter how familiar you are with the terrain." This level of readiness also puts the athlete at mental ease when a competition approaches because there is a reduction of doubt. Most injuries occur from trying to do too much too soon for the body to make proper adaptation. Think of the athletes you know that develop shin splints or another problem because they had to rush to catch up with their training. By staying continuous, the body is much more ready for the increased work that precedes or follows an upcoming contest.

One simple way to immediately improve your continuity is to get a training partner. One of my all time favorite quotes to support this is Proverbs 27:17, "Just as iron sharpens iron, one man must sharpen another." We all know how difficult it is to work out alone. Even if you get a partner, however, there are four main characteristics that he must possess. First, he must be at the same level or higher than you. To work out with an inferior athlete just because he is your friend is only going to lead to decreased performance. Second, he must have similar goals. If the goals are not similar, it is going to be difficult for each of you to motivate each other to stay persistent toward your goal. Third, the partner must live relatively close to you. Excuses like not feeling like driving there or they have things to do back home will become common the farther apart the two of you are. The fourth characteristic is that the two of you should have similar schedules. It is no good if one of you works nights and the other days. The schedules must be similar so there is always a set time to train together. Just think about it, if you really want to skip the workout today, and your partner doesn't have similar needs or your partner lives far away, he may let you off the hook. This will lead to a lack of continuity. An excellent training partner would come to your house, get you out of bed and drag you to train.

Another common problem with athletes I train is that they do not have Continuity in their intensity of training. One day they may train at the correct level of intensity, and other days they may quit early, or work less hard. There are two mental techniques I use on the athletes to combat a lack of consistent training. First, I let them know that I understand that consistently training at a high level of intensity is hard, and I challenge them to understand one thing about their training. I tell them that an hour after their

workout, whether they worked at the correct intensity or not, they are going to feel the same. The workout is going to be over. What they do during that workout is going to determine their long term results. By forgetting their pain and focusing on the goals, they will not let themselves down. If this doesn't work, I use the second, more harsh technique. This is best performed in front of other athletes. I tell them not to worry because their main competition is doing what they are not, so at least there will be a decisive winner. (This one almost always works to enhance the training session.)

Most people are afraid of change. Because of this, training and individual workouts stay relatively the same for long periods of time. This leads to a plateau in performance and boredom. This then leads to a lack continuity and less ability for the athlete to reach his or her full potential. Don't be afraid to mix up your training. Read everything you can get your hands on. Talk to other athletes and coaches. Try a new gym or experience a new training style. This is the way to combat boredom and improve performance. A good rule of thumb that I use here is that you should try to hold yourself to changing your workout completely every 4-6 workouts. This way you are always doing something new and making progress. This will be covered in more detail during the Principle of Variety.

I used the example of the rubbing of Howard's Rock at the beginning of this article to demonstrate how every rub over the decades has had purpose. No matter how small they seemed at the time, everything is added together to help produce the final result. Every rep, set, exercise and workout you choose from now on must be looked at in the same way. You must make sure each one must be as productive and consistent as possible to someday produce the results you want to achieve. You have to make

everything count. You cannot worry about the past or the future. You can only do something about today. That is your gift. That is why they call it the present.

There is an old Brazilian Rhyme that sums up The Principle of Continuity best:

"Agua mole, pedra dura, tanto bate ate que fura"

This is loosely translated to mean, "Soft water, hard rock, but one drop at a time will eventually wear a hole through."

CHAPTER 15

The Principle of Progressive Overload

Progress is life. From birth until death, we are all following a progression. We progress in many different ways throughout our lives: in size, in age, in knowledge, in skill, etc. A training partner of mine says, "If you are not moving forward, then you are dying." I believe that if you look at progression and this statement, it is true. Humans have a need for advancement in life. That is why we have come so far in the last 100 years.

Progress is also a skill. If you do things correctly, you can progress much faster than by making mistakes. Human progress is usually attained by understanding the mistakes made by others and building on them, not making them again. Unfortunately, some aspects of progress in human life are not as well understood as others. No where is this more true than when we examine the process of progression and athletics.

When one thinks of progression in training, one could also call that progression adaptation. Picture your body as an organism composed of billions of cells that work together to make you what you are. Each one of those cells has the ability to adapt to a stimulus. If the stimulus is presented correctly and often enough, there will eventually be a favorable adaptation (progression). If the stimulus is too strong or not often enough, there may be no adaptation that takes place. To demonstrate this, an athlete that lifts correctly on his legs for a month will force the cells of the muscles, tendons, ligaments and bones to adapt to be stronger and more prepared for that activity than they were before they started. The athlete that does too much too soon cannot allow enough time for adaptation to occur and an injury and regression can result. The proper application of

the right weight at the right time with the right amount of recovery is called Progressive Overload. This chapter is going to examine Progressive Overload and allow you to skip the mistakes made by others to properly progress toward your goals.

Progressive Overload is not a new idea. For instance, the most famous example of Progressive Overload is the story of Milo of Crotona. Milo was a famous Greek wrestler that was supposed to have lived in the 6th century B.C.. He was Olympic champion in wrestling 6 times in ancient Greece and was famous for his incredible feats of strength. Milo used Progressive Overload by lifting and carrying a calf every day. After four years of this, the calf grew into a full grown bull, and Milo was able to carry the bull the length of the Olympic Stadium. As you can see, Milo's body adapted to the slow but steady growth of the bull.

Now you may be saying, "If this Principle really worked, then there would be people lifting bulls around and people benching 1000 pounds all over the world." You are right, there are genetic limits to the progression that a human can achieve in strength and speed. The understanding of this Principle is going to help you get as close to those limits as possible. This chapter is going to explain the concepts of Progressive Overload.

As I already stated, a cell is only going to adapt (progress) from a new stimulus. First you must understand that that may be a current exercise that is heavier, done for more reps, done for more sets, done with less rest, done at a different speed, or it could be a different exercise altogether. As you may be shocked by this, there are many ways to change your exercise to achieve a progression.

After you have chosen your new stimulus, you must then use it a certain number of times to achieve long lasting changes (results). You see, if you switch to new

exercises too often, your body will never have the opportunity (time) to change. A good rule of thumb is that the less trained the athlete is, the less often he has to change the exercises. The more advanced the athlete is, the quicker his body adapts and the sooner the exercises have to be changed. For instance, a beginner could do the same routine for 5 months and continue to make progress, while an advanced athlete could begin to plateau after only 5 workouts. By recording your workouts as stated in previous chapters, you will be able to chart progress, and know when it your time (individualization) to move on.

Another good thing to know is how much to progress increases in weight. A common mistake by athletes is increasing the weight too much too soon and not achieving the best results. Science has found that muscles can only gain about 2-4% strength per week. So, once an athlete is trained, expecting increases higher than this may be overshooting the body's ability to adapt. The biggest area to find wrong weights chosen is on exercises where the weights are lighter. For instance if a young athlete curls the 10 pound dumbbells for 8 reps and then the next week tries the 15's, he is probably not going to get eight. This is due to the fact that even though the increase doesn't sound like much it is a 50% increase in weight! That is why I always want my athletes to think in percentages. If you bench 300 pounds for 1 rep and want to see improvement, don't try for 330, which is a 10% increase, but try to get 305 which is less than 2% and in the acceptable range.

A very important piece of training that I have alluded to in other chapters is recovery. Recovery is the time that allows the adaptation of the body to occur. Without proper recovery, proper progress can never occur. This is another area often abused by

athletes. Good rules of thumb to follow here are that most muscles need 5-7 days or more to completely heal, and smaller muscles recover faster than bigger ones. This is why you could hit your biceps (arms) more often than the quadriceps (legs). An insightful way to examine recovery time specifically to your athlete is to record workouts and see if progress in being made. This way, you can find the specific time that the athlete takes to recover and use this time to develop his specific workouts to optimize his training time. If there is not enough time for recovery, injury often occurs. These are usually called overuse injuries and are a great tool for athletes to know when they have gone too far and done too much too soon.

Whenever there is a plateau or injury in training, progress has stopped. When progress is stopped, someone, somewhere is getting ahead of you. By using the knowledge of the Principle of Progressive Overload as a weapon, you should now be able to combat poor training and make more progress than you have before. One of the greatest athletic coaches known in modern day is Vince Lombardi. He was one of the most successful coaches, not just for all of the championships he won, but because he made all of his athletes better people in the process. Vince Lombardi is quoted very often by many coaches today in the United States. He has so many inspiring quotes that it is difficult to pick out a favorite. One that I think is the most appropriate for this chapter is "One must not hesitate to innovate and change with the times. The leader who stands still is not progressing, and he will not remain a leader for long." This statement can easily be applied to take this wisdom, but don't just apply it to your athletics, apply it to every aspect of your life.

CHAPTER 16

The Principle of Variety

Adaptation is an essential part of life. Adaptation can be defined as adjustment to a change in stimuli or circumstance. An athlete is in constant adjustment because nothing ever remains the same for long. Whether it is from workout to workout or season to season, we are constantly undergoing change. By correctly utilizing The Principle of Variety, athletes can properly alter their training programs to adapt to their current needs for progress. The need for change should be recognized, welcomed and readily adapted to in our lives. As a coach of many athletes, however, I rarely see athletes prepared to experience new methods of training. They are unable to recognize decreased gains occurring or the time to enact new methods, but when they do see it is time to mix things up they rarely have the wisdom or the courage to adapt. When I see this reluctance to adapt in my athletes, I use this parable to help them to discover the correct answer of how they should alter not only their training, but also other aspects of their lives as well.

There was once a tribe of nomads that traveled through the desert. The tribe was always on the move because they were always in search of water. Although the tribe traveled together, the tribe was split into two different factions. The factions often disagreed on certain topics, but they worked together to find water to keep each other alive. The tribesman became very good at finding water in the desert. By using the method of trial and error over the years, they were great at what they did. Their methods were a combination of science and instinct, and their thirst kept them driven toward the success of finding water. One day, the tribe found a massive well of water. The well was larger than anything they had ever seen. The large amount of water allowed the tribe to

settle in the area. They first pitched tents, and after a period of time there, they built homes as well. They began to get very comfortable with their well. The tribe got so comfortable that they did not notice when the well began to run dry. They had been there for so long, they forgot to continue to monitor the well. Then one day, the well ran dry. The first faction of the tribe began packing their things as they had in the past because they felt it was time to move on to find more water. The second faction sat and confused themselves with what to do. This is known as paralysis by analysis. They didn't want to move because since the well had water once, surely it would have water again. They didn't even really remember what it was like to search for water anymore. The second faction decided to stay and wait it out, while the first faction moved on. The first tribe found water here and there, and moved throughout the desert once again. The second faction grew weaker from thirst everyday until they couldn't venture out for water even if they tried. Eventually, the second faction perished. The first faction continued to thrive with their movement and even developed new ways of finding and keeping water that made their work easier.

The first question I ask my athletes when they are stagnating and resistant to change is, "What faction of the tribe are you in? The one that adapts and finds a better way, or the one that keeps going to the empty well?" They usually have a breakthrough and see that it is time to move on from the old ways. All types of training will work for a while, but nothing will work forever. With success, many athletes become complacent, and then refuse to use new methods because of the success they once achieved with the old ones. An athlete must often use trial and error as well as instinct to adapt to the current situation. This method can be stressful, because there may be times that new

methods are not working, and the athlete will want to revert back to the old. By realizing that he is making progress even in failure, the athlete should continue on. Training requires constant assessment, because something may really be working well at the time, but recognizing it won't forever will help you look for new methods sooner. If an athlete only focuses on the old aspects of training, he is never going to experience the new. By adding variety to one's training, it becomes harder to be outdated.

As I have written before, the body is simply an organism that adjusts to a variety of stimuli. If the stimulus stays the same for too long, there is no longer any adaptation that takes place. Not only does this make sure there will be no progress, but also boredom is bound to set in. This can lead to decreased desire to train and an eventual decrease in performance. Variety in your training also constantly forces you to question and learn from your training. The trial and error process will help you to eventually form your own training philosophy as well as end your closemindedness to new ideas. A great example of flexibility of thinking is illustrated in the old Chinese story of the reed and the mighty oak tree. The mighty oak laughed at the reed because of its size and stature. The reed, however, continued to follow its own path and was unphased by the hard comments of the oak. One day a terrible storm with high speed winds hit the area where the trees stood. When it passed, the oak was on its side and the reed still stood. The mighty oak could not understand. The reed then explained that you must bend and adjust to the situation and you will return even stronger. To only resist will eventually lead to your demise.

Variety in training can be obvious or subtle. The athlete could use an entirely different workout or the same workout with different repetitions. Both of these would be

examples of change. Other ways to add variety to the workouts could be to change the sets, rest periods, or the tempo of the lifts. One could also experiment with changing the order of the lifts during a workout or even the frequency of the workouts per week. By mixing these simple parameters in your workouts, you are constantly changing the stimulus sent to your body, and the body is forced to adapt. This constant adaptation is how continuous progress is made.

As for changing entire workouts, the rate of adaptation is different depending on the level of athlete that you are. For instance, a beginner can continue with a similar program for weeks or even months and still make gains. An advanced athlete, however, could have already plateaued within just 4 workouts. Knowing this, an athlete must always assess progress and use instinct to help decide when it is time to move on to another well. If you move on too fast, you could miss out on some gains; but if you wait too long, the well may have already run dry.

Another way I add variety to training is to work on correcting imbalances at certain joints. Many of the athletes I have trained train certain lifts and certain parts of the body more than others. This can lead to imbalances, injuries and possible lowered performances. For instance, in America, the bench press is a major lift for many of the athletes. Most feel to improve this lift you must concentrate on the bench press itself. I, however, focus on the stabilizing and antagonistic muscles to improve this lift. Oftentimes I can add 30 pounds to an athlete's lift without ever touching the bench. By focusing on and strengthening the other muscles that are used in the lift but commonly not trained, you increase the overall strength of the athlete. Great examples of exercises would be pull ups, rotator cuff dumbbell work and front dumbbell raises. If these areas

were the weak link in the chain and you continue to avoid them, they will always shut down at the same point and progress will be halted. Add this variety of exercises to your training, allow for more strength to be developed, and you will be on your way to personal records.

A very popular way to add variety to training is cross training. This involves the addition of other sports such as sprinting, swimming, or biking to help develop the conditioning for your particular event. This method definitely decreases boredom, and can add to strength and stamina that an athlete may not have possessed. The athlete must remember, however, that these events are just training tools, and that their main event must still be the primary focus. The fighter that likes to run or bike must remember that fighting is still the training event that requires the most attention. There is often no substitute for your actual event.

The parable of the well told at the beginning of this chapter forces the athlete to adapt or die. Look back on your career and visualize how many times you have gone back to the empty well hoping for a little of that old magic. Think back when you were resistant to trying new things. Store those images as lessons, or even write them down as a reminder. The wisdom that you gain from these lessons will insure that you will never find yourself thirsty again.

CHAPTER 17

The Principle of Proper Nutrition

The younger athletes I see today have a tough road laid out for them when it comes to nutrition. With fast food joints hammering them with advertising, to the lack nutrient dense food for them to eat, to an increased sedentary lifestyle not adding up to their food portion size, eating well is a difficult decision. I call it a decision, because we all have a choice. That choice should, but unfortunately does not often begin with education. If you have ever walked in a supermarket, 90% of the place has no nutritional value. Yet, every product in the place will tell you how good it is for you and how packed it is with vitamins. Who are we to believe? If it's fat free, then it's got to be good, right? During the following principle, I am not going to bombard you with specific nutrition information. Instead I am going to deliver techniques and strategies that may assist you in following this principle more closely.

Whenever I cover the topic of nutrition at a seminar, I always begin by asking the audience what vehicle would they drive if they could drive the car of their wildest dreams. I hear answers ranging from Ferrari to Porsche to Bentley. People always have a smile when they give their answers as if they are proud to think so grandiose. Some even name the color or year the car would have to be as well. People take pride in such a complex and stylish machine. I then ask the audience, "If you were to take this car and pull up to the gas station, what type of gas would you select?" The resounding answer is always the best that they offer, of course. I then let them in on a little secret. The best vehicle they will ever have is their body. In fact, if science were able to build their body and make it work, it would cost billions of dollars to make happen. I ask them if they are

truthfully putting the best gas in this vehicle. Most of the heads usually drop at this time, and the point is well taken.

Without your health, you have nothing. If you are ill, you cannot enjoy any of the things many people place above sound nutrition in a hierarchy of importance. I believe that food is our greatest medicine. When used correctly, many problems such as diabetes, obesity, high blood pressure and others would dramatically decrease. Instead of always looking for the pill to easily fix the problem, remove the poor eating habits and you don't need the pill. I know this is easier said than done, but until people realize the importance of their health and its relationship to nutrition, most people just look for the quick fix to make the resultant problems disappear.

Eating well first requires education. That is the first step that most of the American population is missing. That is the step that would alleviate many of the health problems that exist today. The problem with nutrition education is where the information you view comes from. If it is on a box of high fructose corn syrup covered sugar pops, you may still feel you are learning something valuable. A great place to start is with a nutritionist or a registered dietician. If you simply don't know how many calories you need in a day, then everything you do from that point is just guesswork. Seek out information not only about calories, but what are the best sources to derive those calories from. Once you understand the sources and their caloric content, you will better be able to select a portion size. Then understanding how to split those calories and portion sizes into meals throughout the day will help you to plan your diet in advance.

Beside education, I am also making the assumption that the essential characteristic of discipline is firmly in place at this time as well. Nowhere does a lack of

discipline run rampant than when it comes to nutrition. I have over the years, been given a few tools which can help to put you on the right track to following purposeful nutrition. My first boss, Larry Bock was a nutrition freak. Not only was everything right down to the calorie and portion size, all of his food was organically grown and pesticide and hormone free. One Monday at work, I was talking about eating a number of hot dogs at the Jets game the day before. He stopped me in the middle of my story and asked me to imagine that hot dog becoming part of every cell of my body. He asked if that was what I really wanted to do. Picture the components of what is in a hot dog becoming one with you. The technique really stuck with me. I guess it was his way of better expressing the old slogan, "You are what you eat." Today, I can't eat or watch someone eat something terrible for them without thinking about it. This example and the questioning about the car have been tools to help me get athletes on the path to better discipline.

Another great technique my boss taught me was something he called Zen eating. Larry liked to enjoy his food, while I would just wolf mine down and get back to what I was doing. I learned to eat slowly and enjoy everything about what I was eating from the taste to the sound to the texture. This slower eating habit allows you to savor your food more completely and fill you before you are engorged from eating too fast. I further expanded on this technique to help me enjoy things that may not have been the best things to eat without going too far. I have eaten just about everything I can think of. To me, therefore, why do I have to eat tons of something that I have already had. For instance, I can enjoy a bite of chocolate and still feel I had some. This still allows you to enjoy in food pleasures and helps you to have the discipline to not go too far.

Many of the questions I field every day revolve around supplements. From when should an athlete begin using creatine to how much protein should be in their shake, everyone is always looking for the new miracle supplement. I think supplements have come a long way in the last number of years. Just walk into a Vitamin Shoppe or a General Nutrition Center and you can easily be overwhelmed with the myriad of choices. Before I answer anything to an athlete about supplements, though, I always ask them one question, "How good is your diet?" The answer is almost always, "Not so good." This is when I use an example I first heard from my colleague Joe DeFranco. He states that just like you must put on your shirt before you put on your tie, you must first eat well before you ever entertain the possibilities of supplements. We are both amazed at the athletes that will spend thousands of dollars per year on different supplements, yet their diet is all but junk. If you are thinking about what the next best supplement is to buy, first ask yourself if you are putting your shirt or your tie first. If it is the tie, you are going to look pretty silly up at the counter of GNC.

Another concept that I submit to all my athletes is that an athlete has very different requirements than a non athlete. An athlete's life is about performance. Due to this fact, an athlete must eat to perform. I especially experience trouble in this area when dealing with female athletes. They are usually under pressure for both performance and aesthetics. This commonly forces them to limit themselves according to their specific needs. By letting them know that they have to eat to perform, many instantly find justification and have a release of the fears about how much or what they might be eating.

Go out and seek the nutritional information you are looking for. I will admit this is often the most difficult principle to follow. Just refer back to your goals and use the

techniques described above, and you should be on the path to better eating. As my mentor and friend Bill Parisi always tells me, "If you have a big enough why, you will eventually figure out how."

CHAPTER 18

The Principle of Recovery and Restoration

One of the biggest breakthroughs I had later in my athletic career was realizing how important recovery was to success as well as the fact that recovery had many specific forms that could be manipulated. Looking back on my own sports career, I often play the "what if" game when it comes to the application of adequate recovery and restoration techniques.

I was always a person that burned the candle at both ends. I trained hard, I studied hard, and I made sure I had fun hard as well. The problem with that hard athletic lifestyle is that one has a hard time fitting in recovery. Add this to the fact that recovery and restoration is another concept that everyone understands, but rarely applies, and you know performance is bound to suffer somewhere down the line.

Even though I can say that my own lack of understanding of recovery could have lead to past failures, I do feel it is the responsibility of a coach or mentor to have good working knowledge of this principle in addition to all of the others. Unfortunately, when this knowledge is limited to "ice the leg down" or "get plenty of sleep," mistakes in training are bound to happen. Hopefully the following story will allow you not to make the same error I did.

A number of years back, I had spent 6 straight months training for the US Bobsled team while I was finishing my physical therapy school residency. I was doing what I would consider a number of things in alignment with the characteristics and principles that I had developed up until that point. For instance, I was studying and understood my speed and strength training, I developed and was recording every periodized workout set

to my specific needs, I was training economically, I was resting and I was eating well. The summer before Bobsled testing began I knew I was in my best shape up until that date. I performed well at the test and decided to stay at the Olympic Training Center the rest of the summer to enhance my chances of success for making one of the top teams. Unfortunately, this was the point that things began to break down. In order to rightfully stay at the center, the athletes had to work out every day. I was a hard worker, so I had no problem with that. The problem lay in the fact that I violated almost every principle I centered myself around once I was there. The programs for all of the athletes were the same, my diet went into the dumps, and worst of all, the workouts each day were almost identical. We performed sprints, jumps, and sled pushes every day for weeks. The reason we finally stopped was everyone was either injured or just plain neurologically crushed. I went from my best numbers to receiving cortisone shots in a big toe I was contemplating cutting off to stop the pain. Even though I felt horrible, my good friend and Olympic Silver medalist Todd Hays seemed to enjoy my experience. Needless to say, I did not perform as well as I would have liked, and now I have grown from the event. This was actually a stepping stone to set the concepts of this book in motion. Now you must take advantage of the lesson before the mistake occurs.

When I used to think about recovery, I defined the concept as taking a long enough period of time doing nothing until you were ready to do something again. Now I know and insist that you view the concept with much more respect. Recovery can be an important passive process such as sleeping or the avoidance of drugs and alcohol, but it is often an active procedure that requires great attention. For instance, some of the major active applications of recovery I use with my athletes is either self or therapist massage,

icing, numerous forms of stretching, hot and cold water treatments (hydrotherapy), “feeder workouts”, proper nutrition and supplementation, biofeedback, and yoga. These recovery techniques require effort, time, and an understanding of their importance to overall performance. Because these are often limited commodities when it comes to athletes, recovery is usually confined to simply not working out.

I am going to now describe some of the recovery techniques that have worked best for me and my athletes in the past. By no means am I saying these are the only ones that work or the only ones to try out. I am also not going to go into the science or theory of why they work. These choices are just from personal experience and are being described to demonstrate the number of different forms of recovery that are out there.

Icing and different forms of hydrotherapy have always resulted in advanced recovery for me. For instance, I am regimented in icing any body part that is troublesome for a number of hours per day until that problem subsides. I like to use a plastic bag filled with ice and water wrapped in another ice bag or two to prevent leaking. I leave the bag on for twenty minutes and switch to another area of concern for twenty more while that area reheats. I repeat this process for at least one hour.

Cold bath is an excellent form of post workout recovery methodology if you have the luxury of a cold bath. This is a test of wills, especially the more of your body you choose to submerge in the icy depths. In terms of temperature, I find around 50 degrees to be tolerable. Staying in for five to ten minutes is usually my limit. This can be contrasted with a hot bath which really gets the circulation following. The temperature will feel hotter than it is at first. I like to repeat the process for a few cycles and always finish with hot. If the bath is unavailable, a shower is the next best thing. The contrast

method can be used here as well, but it is tough to blast yourself with the cold water and still stand under the spray. This type of shower is great following a strenuous workout and should focus on the specific areas hit during the training session.

As for massage, I believe it is a powerful recovery technique. Unfortunately, not every athlete can afford such measures. If this is the case, self massage works great as well. The shower is an excellent opportunity to perform this immediately following a workout. I always instruct my athletes to massage the muscles in the direction back to the heart. This return of blood flow and relaxing of the musculature has had many athletes swear by the advanced recovery results.

Finally, I will discuss nutrition again, but in terms of recovery. Obviously, overall diet is critical to an athlete's recovery potential, but I place extra value on post workout nutrition in terms of immediate recovery impact. I believe that post workout nutrition is the most important meal an athlete can have in a day. I like that meal in liquid form (shake), with a ratio of carbohydrates to protein that is required by the type of training that just occurred. Oftentimes, this is around a 4 to 1 ratio. I like the carbohydrates to be composed of glucose polymers and the protein to be whey. Antioxidants are also a must, with a helping of L Glutamine of at least 2 grams. Following this formula, find the taste you like, but make sure you have the shake immediately after the workout. Recovery is best promoted this way.

The Principle of Recovery is the last principle covered in this book. I have found that only once an athlete is centered around the other ten principles, that athlete can then understand and apply recovery completely. As I have stated throughout this text, an athlete must try to apply all of the eleven principles to help guide purposeful training.

One can view these unchanging principles as a compass. They will help to give you direction when questions arise. A final exercise would be to apply the ten previous principles to recovery and try to determine an adequate recovery method for yourself at your certain point in your training. The progression of examining recovery with application of the ten previous principles can be explained as follows.

By utilizing the Principle of Understanding, one could deduce that there have to be specific methods of recovery that are best for certain people depending on age, gender, sport and competitive level. This would support the Principle of Individualization in that what recovery methods work for one athlete may not work for another. Without first using light general methods of recovery, the Principle of a Solid Foundation would not allow one to go to immediate drastic or advanced methods. Following this general approach, and athlete could then use the Principle of Specialization to select the specific method of recovery that best fits the exact need at that time. An athlete's recovery process would have to be planned and recorded. This statement would be in direct support of the Principle of Periodization. One must utilize the Principle of Training Economy to select the most time effective method of recovery at that time. The Principle of Continuity dictates that recovery has to stay constant throughout training to ever truly reap any of its benefits. I have already stated during the Principle of Progressive Overload that the body is just an organism that responds to the stimuli presented to it. The body adapts to that stimulus to then be prepared to accept that stimulus if it is ever presented again. The Principle of Recovery further adds to this statement in that the adaptation needs to have adequate time to take place. This time can be cut down slightly with the active techniques already described, but can only be so physiologically fast. By

also understanding the Principle of Variety, one can easily conclude that no recovery method will work for long, and proper choice of the proper recovery method at the correct time is essential. Finally, recovery could not be complete without the application of the Principle of Proper Nutrition. Nutrition is a major method used by all successful athletes today to manipulate recovery and restoration.

Throughout my athletic and coaching career, I was constantly bombarded with the newest and latest trend whether it be technique, supplement, or device. This book is my answer to the question of how to sift through that bombardment. Experience has given me confidence in these principles, but you must experience them for yourself and make your own decisions. Just as I opened the book with the idea that many people just follow the scripts of someone else, you cannot now just accept mine. Question everything and everyone. Take what you feel works, and discard what you feel does not. That is the only way you are going to develop real knowledge. Training to me is a process of trial and error followed by recording and re-evaluation. By utilizing a similar sequential application of the eleven principles on any aspect of your training, you should be able to make proper decisions regarding the path to take that is the best fit for you at that specific time.

CHAPTER 19

Conclusion

Each week the Parisi Speed School offers what is known as the Orientation to our program. The purpose behind this hour and a half lecture is to introduce parents and athletes to our program, allow them to see the facility, and educate them a little bit about training and sports. After they have gone through the Orientation, they will have a better idea if they want to get involved with our program or not. What I have found interesting over the years of giving this seminar is that all people understand something about the principles of training. The problem is that most of what they know is either myth or false. I think it is puzzling that everyone finds out the same myths and buys into them. I guess that is why so many fitness products in the U.S. sell, even though most of them are junk, and end up as an expensive clothes hanger. It is almost as if many people are just born with some false ideas about fitness. I have spent years of training and experimenting with athletes to try to find the truths about training. Every time I get a chance to speak in front of large groups, I try to expose them to the principles contained in this book to guide them in the right direction.

I begin every orientation by asking every athlete their name and the sport that they play. Then I tell them that I am going to first ask them a bunch of questions and the only rules are that they cannot answer the same way as the person before them, and they cannot say "I don't know." After these instructions, I go around the room asking each athlete why he or she came to see me that day. Usually the first set of answers is, "To get faster" or "To get stronger." After I get this initial line of answers, I then ask, "And why is that important?" Many of the athletes look at me strangely, and then the usual answers are things like, "To be a better player," "To make a certain team," or "To be the

best I can be." I then tell them what good answers those were, but ask them again in order, "And why is that important?" Now some of the kids are getting stumped. The answers come much more slowly at this point. The next line of answers usually follows as, "To get into a good college," "To be recognized and remembered as a good player," or "To eventually make money." After this set of answers, I smile at them because they know what is coming next. "And why is it important to go to a good college?" "And why is it important to be recognized?" "And why is it important to have money?" Usually here is where athletes have a hard time answering and the "I don't knows" start to come out.

I take a second to let the athletes realize that they have not really thought out their plan for athletics, or even why they are doing athletics at all. Then I help put them on the path to the answer. "How would you FEEL if you got stronger and faster in our program?" The answer is an overwhelming "Good!" "And how would you FEEL if you became a better player?" The answer is now "Really Good!" "And how would you FEEL if you were eventually rich and recognized as a great athlete?" Now the answer moves to "Great!"

This is when I let the athletes know they are now onto something. They did not come to visit me to get faster or stronger. They did not come to hear me speak to be a better player. They also did not come to eventually make money. What they really came for is to feel better about themselves. To make themselves feel good. What I find interesting is that in all of the years of doing that orientation, I have never had an athlete come up with the answer. I think we are caught up in the immediate results that we forget the real reason we ever chose to do a sport in the first place. Science demonstrates

that humans will most often do things for one of two reasons: Either to feel good or to not feel bad. So you see, either way, we are always in the direction of good. Think how much harder you will work knowing that the end result will help you to feel great about yourself. Think about how much easier it will be to wake up for an early practice or eat the right things when you know it is going to help you feel better.

It took me many years to come to the conclusion that all the suffering I put myself through was to eventually make me feel good. When people asked me why I trained in pain or didn't slip in my diet, it was because I knew I liked the results more than I liked that piece of food. I knew I was going to feel better about myself.

Now feeling better about yourself can also send you down the wrong path as well. For instance, most people overeat because the eating makes them feel good. Many people don't work out because they do not want to feel sore and bad. Now this immediate gratification, unfortunately, will not last forever. Even though the bad food and not working out make the person feel good then, the results will eventually not allow them to feel good about themselves. Actually it is going to help them to feel bad. This example should help you to examine the results of what you are thinking about doing at all times when it comes to your training, your eating, or just about anything in your life. Ask yourself, "Is what I am about to do going to eventually help me to feel better about myself?" If you cannot justify a good answer for this, perhaps this is not what you really want to do. Don't succumb to immediate gratification if you now have the wisdom to see through to the end result.

In conclusion, you did not read this book because you had to for a class or because you wanted to get a little smarter. You read this book because somehow the

knowledge contained inside is going to allow you to feel better about yourself. When you finally realize this and apply this lesson to everything you are doing, that is when you will be truly successful. I have met many athletes and people with more money than you could imagine and they were not happy. I have met athletes that were still playing their sport even though the feeling they used to get from it was now gone. I have met people with jobs that other people were very envious of. And yet these people were all not happy. So others looking from the outside might consider all of these people a success, but I do not. Having what others consider a great life is not success, living a life that makes you feel good every day is. So you should now see that asking the question, "And why is that important?" is not just a way to enhance your training or athletic career, it is a way to enhance your quality of life.

Refer to this book whenever you have questions about your training. Hopefully, the characteristics and principles provided will give you the direction you seek. My final piece of advice is as follows:

If you want to create a program that will allow you to enjoy success and happiness as an athlete, you must do 3 things: First, figure out and live by your core values of being an athlete. Second, center yourself around the principles provided in this text. And finally, don't just train, TRAIN TO WIN!

References

Andzel, W., Lisky, M. *Fitness for the New Millennium.* Iowa: Kendall/Hunt. 1998.

Beckwith, H. *Selling the Invisible.* New York: Warner Books, Inc. 1997.

Covey, S. *The 7 Habits of Highly Effective People.* New York: Fireside. 1990.

Drabik, J. *Children and Sports Training.* Vermont: Stadion. 1996.

Francis, C. *Training for Speed.* Australia: Faccioni Speed & Conditioning. 1997.

Hartmann, J., Tunnemann H. *Fitness and Strength Training for All Sports.* Canada: Sports Books Publishers. 2000.

Hatfield, F. *Power: A Scientific Approach.* Illinois: Contemporary Books. 1989.

King, I. *How to Write Strength Training Programs.* Australia: King Sports. 2000.

Kurz, T. *Science of Sports Training: How to Plan and Control Training for Peak Performance.* Vermont: Stadion. 2001.

Maxwell, J. *Failing Forward.* Tennessee: Thomas Nelson, Inc. 2000.

Millman, D. *The Inner Athlete.* New Hampshire: Stillpoint. 1994.

Poliquin, C. *The Poliquin Principles.* California: Dayton Publications. 1997.

Siff, M. *Fact and Fallacies of Fitness.* Colorado: Self Published. 2000.

Siff, M., Verkhoshansky, Y. *Supertraining.* Colorado: Self Published. 1999.

Staley, C. *The Science of Martial Arts Training.* California: Multi-Media Books. 1999.

Starzynski, T., Sozanski, H. *Explosive Power and Jumping Ability for All Sports.* Vermont: Stadion. 1999.

Zatsiorsky, V. *Science and Practice of Strength Training.* Illinois: Human Kinetics. 1995.

About the Author

Martin Rooney is a Performance Enhancement Specialist with a Master of Health Science and Bachelor of Physical Therapy from the Medical University of South Carolina. He also holds a Bachelor of Arts in Exercise Science from Furman University.

Martin was a member of the United States Bobsled team from 1995-1997, 2000 and a four-time All Conference, MVP performer in Track and Field at Furman.

Martin is a Certified Strength and Conditioning Specialist under NSCA and a member of the Society of Weight Training Injury Specialists. He is also a certified in Active Release Technique for the upper extremity and certified in the lower extremity by the Institute of Flexibility Sciences. He also currently writes for the Elite Fitness Systems Website and is a columnist for Brazil's Gracie Magazine.

Martin has lectured for the American College of Sports Medicine and has been commissioned by Nike to run speed testing camps at a number of major universities. He has also coauthored two other books on the forty yard dash and the vertical jump. He has traveled as far as the Middle East to train in the United Arab Emirates as well as to help prepare fighters in Japan.

Currently, Martin is the director of the Parisi Speed School in Fair Lawn, NJ. Martin has been a speed consultant to the New York Giants as well as other athletes from the NFL, MLB, NBA, WNBA and numerous top Division I colleges across the country. He has also trained Olympians including one gold, and one silver medalist. In addition to this, Martin also trains some of the top mixed martial artists in the world.

Over the last few years Martin has helped to develop one of the top NFL combine training programs in the country producing the fastest athlete at the 2001 NFL Combine and first place finishers at eight different positions, including three all-time records.

Martin is married and lives in Fair Lawn, NJ. He and his wife, Amanda, are expecting their first child a few months from the time this book was written.

Contact Info:

For more information about The Parisi Speed School, or to contact Martin Rooney with regards to upcoming seminars, books, videos, etc., please use the information provided below.

The Parisi Speed School
2-22 Banta Place
Fair Lawn, NJ 07410
Phone: 201-794-1555
Fax: 201-794-6009
Website: parisischool.com